The Surf Atlas

Iconic Waves and Surfing Hinterlands

gestalten

4
THE WORLDWIDE JOY RIDE

6
OCEANIA AND THE PACIFIC

8
The Seven-Mile Miracle
North Shore of Oahu, Hawaii, United States

14
In the Belly of the Beast
Jaws, Hawaii, United States

20
A Modern Upwelling
in the Original Surf City
Waikiki, Hawaii, United States

26
RIDE EVERYTHING:
THE LONG AND THE SHORT

34
Agony and Ecstasy
Teahupoo, Tahiti, French Polynesia

42
Tradition Reimagined
in Papua New Guinea
Papua New Guinea

48
New Zealand's Perfect Peninsula
*Coromandel Peninsula,
New Zealand*

54
The Best of the Wild Wild West
Margaret River, Australia

60
Nature's Nastiest Staircase
Shipstern Bluff, Australia

66
AFRICA

68
Tubes at the Tip of Africa
Cape Town, South Africa

76
Racing Widow-Makers
on the Skeleton Coast
Skeleton Bay, Namibia

82
West Africa's Surfing Stronghold
Dakar, Senegal

88
Sampling Ghana's Rhythm and Groove
Ghana

94
Indestructible Stoke
on the Outskirts of Lagos
Tarkwa Bay, Nigeria

102
Treasure and Treachery
in the Fortunate Isles
Canary Islands, Spain

108
Africa's Uncharted Isle
Madagascar

114
ASIA

116
Perpetual Flux in the Philippine Sea
Siargao, Philippines

122
The Surfer's Reverie
Mentawai Islands, Indonesia

128
Taiwan's Green and Pleasant Coast
Taitung, Taiwan

134
Surfing in the Spice Garden
Kerala, India

140
The Pioneering Women
of Iranian Surfing
Ramin, Iran

146
Chasing Mirages in the Empty Quarter
Oman

152
CHASING THE GHOSTS
OF A SURFING DREAM

160
NORTH AMERICA

162
California's Cold Coliseum
Mavericks, United States

170
INCREMENTS OF FEAR IN THE
LAND OF THE GIANTS

178
The First Perfect Wave
Malibu, United States

182
Movers and Shakers on Vancouver Island
Tofino, Canada

188
North America's Fickle Frontier
Alaska, United States

194
CENTRAL AND SOUTH AMERICA

196
Welcome to the Merciless Mex Pipe
Puerto Escondido, Mexico

202
A Shangri-La for the Easy-Going Glider
Nayarit, Mexico

208
STYLE IS EVERYTHING:
THE ART OF SURFING

216
Off the Beaten Track in Costa Rica
Nosara, Costa Rica

222
Panama's Lush Caribbean
Archipelago
Bocas del Toro, Panama

228
Cuban Surfers Fight for Freedom
Cuba

234
A Faithful Quest for Peru's
Endless Left
Chicama, Peru

238
Land of the Left
Pichilemu, Chile

244
Following Surfing's Ancient Throughline
Easter Island, Chile

250
EUROPE

252
Europe's Sleeping Giant
Nazaré, Portugal

258
A Wave for All Seasons
Ericeira, Portugal

262
From Swamp to Silver Coast
Hossegor, France

268
Britain's Rugged Surfing Heartland
Cornwall, England

274
The Magic Energy of the Emerald Isle
West Coast, Ireland

280
Cold Consolations in Caledonia
North Coast, Scotland

286
The Hardcore Surfers of the Hel Peninsula
Hel Peninsula, Poland

290
The Muddy Brothers of the River Severn
The Severn Bore, England

296
Giants, Witches, and Wedges
Faroe Islands, Denmark

302
Viking Treasures in the Far North
Lofoten Islands, Norway

310
SUB-ZERO SURFING IN THE
LANDS OF ICE AND SNOW

318
INDEX

320
IMPRINT

The Worldwide Joy Ride

BY LUKE GARTSIDE

When viewed from outer space, our earth famously appears as a predominantly blue planet, thanks to the vast oceans that cover most of its surface. But if you look closely, you'll find great swathes of that blue frequently obscured by swirls of white—marauding columns of cloud and wind that whip the ocean beneath into a state of kaleidoscopic frenzy. From that chaos, swells emerge, rolling purposefully away from the source, slowly stacking into orderly lines that take on the appearance of fresh corduroy. Eventually, they arrive at one of the land's jagged edges, where the specific geography forces them into breaking waves of all shapes and sizes. Often you'll find a huddle of surfers there. Dark figures against the blue, undulating in restless devotion, eager for a chance to be carried by a parcel of well-traveled storm energy as it spills onto the shore. It's an act so simple in its essence—shared with ancient man, seabirds, dolphins, and even the odd mollusk—but it's one that has come to thoroughly enthrall terrestrial beings over the last century or so. Recent estimates suggest there are now over 20 million surfers worldwide, fanned out across more than 150 countries.

The tales of how surfing spread, took root, and evolved in so many coastal enclaves are as varied as the places themselves. Accounts and artifacts from West Africa, South America, China, and the Pacific suggest wave riding was practiced for many hundreds of years prior to the arrival of modern surfboards. Indeed, it's easy to imagine why a child might have been compelled to grab a bit of floating wood and bounce in on the shore break, or why a canoe-bound fisherman might have sought a ride on the white water for safe and speedy passage to the shore.

As far as we know, however, it was only in ancient Polynesia that surfing gathered enough fervor to transform it from a casual pastime into a cultural powerhouse. In Hawaii in particular, it became a central tenet of community recreation and ritual. Islanders rode standing tall, on a multitude of specially made crafts, incorporating everything from courtship to gambling and status displays into their watery dance.

Modern surfing's march around the globe began in the early twentieth century, led by a pair of Hawaiians; waterman George Freeth and Olympic medal-winning swimmer Duke Kahanamoku. Over the course of a single decade, they introduced the sport to Australia and both coasts of the U.S. mainland with a series of demonstrations attended by hundreds.

New strongholds sprouted in their wake and many years later, it would be from them that surfers emanated to continue the Hawaiians' legacy, seeding the culture in every corner of the map. Propelled by a desire to discover new frontiers and uncrowded lineups—or simply to break from the humdrum of their far-flung military bases—from the 1940s onwards sailors, smugglers, servicepeople, and hippies fleeing the draft formed an unlikely alliance of global surfing ambassadors. Wherever they paddled out, their exploits drew intrigue and whenever boards were left behind, locals were quick to pick them up.

Despite an ability—and indeed a common preference in modern times—to practice the pastime in solitude, early fanatics from these emerging scenes rarely sought isolation. In almost every case, from Rapa Nui to India to Senegal, the first generation of modern surfers were powerfully motivated to welcome others into the fray, usually driven by nothing more than a desire to share the joy of it all. As the surfing bug bit, individual lives were changed overnight, altered by shifting perspectives and new aspirations. Eventually, so too were entire communities. Fresh geographies were laid over the coastline. Rocky outcrops, bits of reef, and sandy shore were suddenly ascribed new names and personalities, transformed from anonymous crags to storied surf breaks. Each attracted a pack of disciples, obsessively dedicated to deciphering their every mood under the various vagaries of tide, wind, and swell. In time, these surfers would become the custodians of their ocean spaces, ready to lead campaigns against any threat, from sewage spill to destructive coastal development.

Usually, at some point in this evolution, surf tourists would flood in, fundamentally altering the place purely with their presence, as on Bali's Bukit Peninsula, or Siargao Island in the Philippines, where once-blighted coastal plots were fast transformed into the region's hottest property thanks to their proximity to coveted waves. For some settlements, the transition to "surf destination" came with great benefits, for others with serious drawbacks and damage, and for most, a liberal helping of each.

Over a century on from the start of the sport's grand expansion, the surfing world has become one of dizzying diversity. From the teeming metropolis to the remote jungle village, the snow-covered beach to the baking equatorial shore, it seems that now almost wherever there are waves, there are surfers. Some are dedicated to pushing their limits in watery mountains the size of five-story buildings. Others are focused on the most effortless traverse of a perfect waist-high peeler. Many consider it a sport, others an art, and some even a means of healing, empowerment, and community cohesion. But wherever you go, all remain united by its universal draw; the simple but supreme pleasure of the ride.

It has often been said that surfing transcends all politics. However, as wave riding reaches ever more distant shores and distinct cultural settings, it has become clear that it isn't always a total escape from the messy business that governs life on land. Lack of equipment, the privatization of the coast, and cultural barriers all play a part in preventing surfers from accessing their waves. It's only by acknowledging these obstacles that we can harness our collective power to help break them down. Fostering connections across cultures is one thing our otherwise beautifully frivolous pastime has always excelled in. Modern surf culture shines in the moments individuals are inspired to stand with their fellow frothers; to donate, campaign, and rally to preserve all the things that really matter to them. Because when you're a surfer—even one from a world away—they're probably the same things that really matter to you too.

Oceania and the Pacific

1 North Shore of Oahu, Hawaii, United States
2 Jaws, Hawaii, United States
3 Waikiki, Hawaii, United States
4 Teahupoo, Tahiti, French Polynesia
5 Papua New Guinea
6 Coromandel Peninsula, New Zealand
7 Margaret River, Australia
8 Shipstern Bluff, Australia

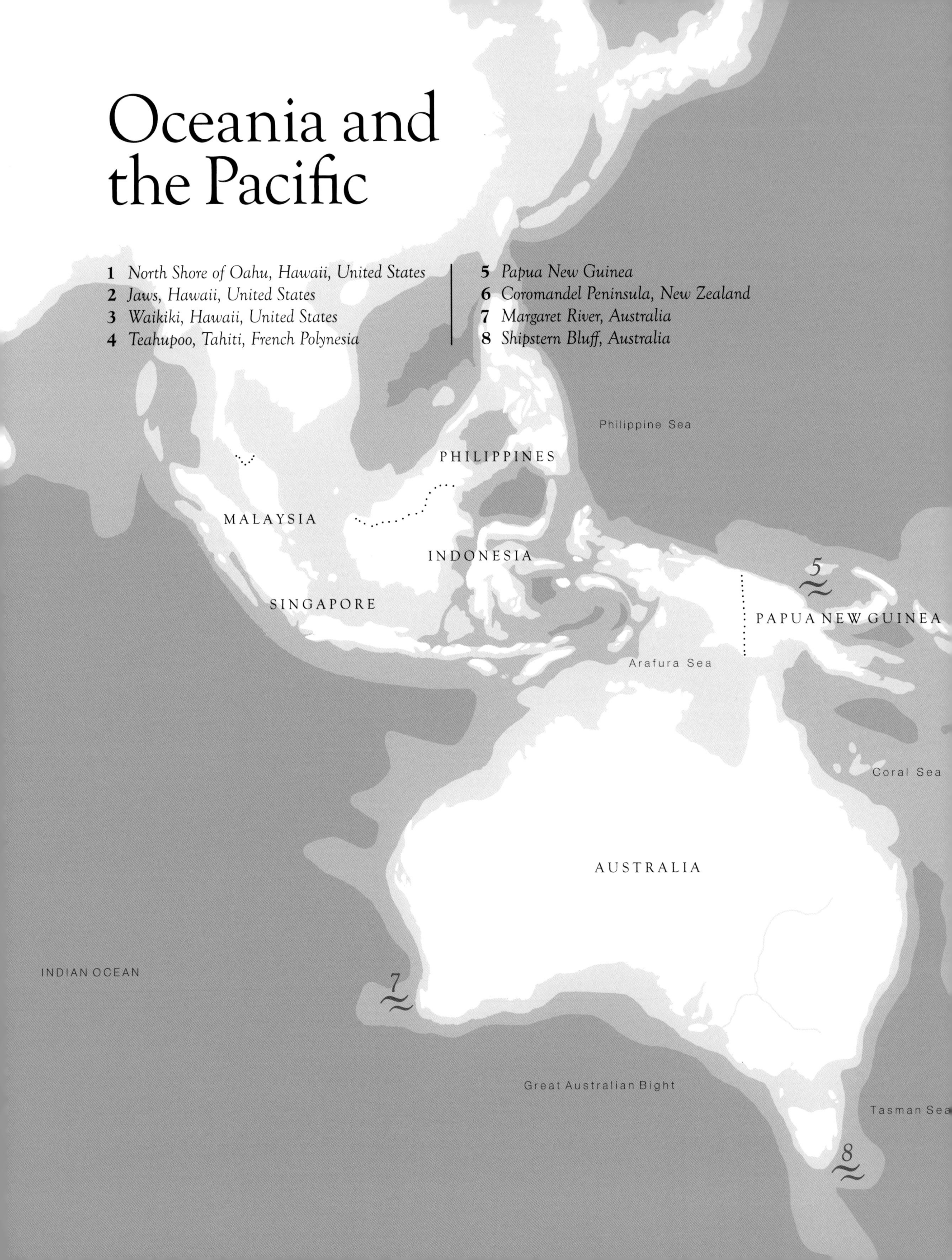

Philippine Sea

PHILIPPINES

MALAYSIA

INDONESIA

5

SINGAPORE

PAPUA NEW GUINEA

Arafura Sea

Coral Sea

AUSTRALIA

INDIAN OCEAN

7

Great Australian Bight

Tasman Sea

8

NORTH PACIFIC OCEAN

HAWAII (UNITED STATES)

TAHITI (FRENCH POLYNESIA)

4

SOUTH PACIFIC OCEAN

6

NEW ZEALAND

The Seven-Mile Miracle

North Shore of Oahu, Hawaii, United States

If surf culture has a Mecca, the North Shore of Oahu is surely it. Centered in the islands that gave birth to the sport as we know it, no surf zone on earth is more historically significant than the seven-mile miracle—a wave-drenched stretch from Haleiwa to Velzyland crammed with over a dozen different breaks.

The epicenter is the Banzai Pipeline, the spiritual home of tube riding. Waves unload here with such ferocity onto a pockmarked blend of coral and hard lava that spectators can feel the beach rumble beneath them. First surfed in the early 1960s, it only truly came to the fore a decade later, thanks to new-fangled shortboards and the groundbreaking approach of local talents like Gerry Lopez, whose incredible skill and serenity in the tube earned him the moniker "Mr. Pipeline." Since then, it's remained the apple of the surfing world's eye, featuring in an endless stream of magazine spreads and iconic movie parts.

Just a stone's throw away, Off the Wall and Backdoor break with the same flawless precision, but in the other direction. Then there's the storied Sunset Beach, whose bowl remains the global benchmark for wave power, and Waimea, a huge right-hander that's been a central pillar of the big wave world for over half a century. The shore break on the inside is equally perilous. Historically avoided at all costs, it now hosts a mix of body-boarders and kamikaze standups, hunting for cavernous barrels right on the sand.

There are high-performance playgrounds at Rocky Point, Log Cabins, and Haleiwa, and for mere surfing mortals, more cruisey peaks at Chun's, Freddyland, and Monster Mush.

Lineups are uber-competitive across the board and governed by a strict set of unwritten rules. While transgressions aren't punished by local heavies as severely as they once were, when paddling for waves, as with crossing the Kam Highway, it's advisable to always look both ways before going. ∼

Murray Antonieff on a beautiful bomb at Waimea Bay (previous spread, right). Leah Dawson plowing her own furrow with a stylish cheater five (above). When Pipeline comes alive, it always draws a hungry pack of elite surfers looking for the wave of their lives (below). A postcard-perfect palm grove at Pua'ena Point (opposite).

What You Need to Know

Level:
Intermediate to expert.

Best time to visit:
The prime window is from November to February, with early or late season promising fewer surfers but still plenty of swells.

What to bring:
You're going to need lots of sunscreen. Choose a reef-safe brand to minimize your impact on the island's delicate marine ecosystems.

What to do when it's flat:
In winter, it's never really flat. But if you're surfed out, you can go turtle watching at Laniakea Beach or visit the Polynesian Cultural Center.

Local tip:
Time a trip to coincide with the Pipeline Masters to witness competitive surfing's greatest spectacle.

The plus to surf:
i. North-West Maui; ii. Big Island

NORTH PACIFIC OCEAN

HAWAII

PAPUA NEW GUINEA

Coral Sea

TAHITI

In the Belly of the Beast

Jaws, Hawaii, United States

Located on the north shore of Maui, the colossal peaks of Jaws (Pe'ahi) have served as ground zero for every breakthrough and sea change in modern big-wave surfing.

The wave's rise to prominence was intimately tied to that of tow surfing in the early 1990s, when a group of Hawaiians used jet skis to propel themselves to previously unfathomable feats. Images of their escapades spread far beyond the surfing sphere, appearing everywhere from the cover of *National Geographic* to the opening sequence of the 2002 Bond film *Die Another Day*. For years, the consensus remained that towing was the only way to tackle Jaws at size. "You can't catch a freight train on a bicycle," explained Darrick Doerner, one of the early pioneers. "You have to match power with power."

However, by the 2010s, opinion had diverged and the wave took center stage in a purist-led paddle-surfing resurgence. Driven by raw skill and innovations in equipment, the new school was able to redefine what was possible on Maui's monster walls once again. Soon, surfers were dropping into waves the size of five-story buildings under arm power alone and while tow surfing would eventually make its comeback, the sport's core values would be forever changed.

Kai Lenny is the most acclaimed waterman on earth, collecting accolades in surfing, stand-up paddle boarding (above), and various wind sports. Recently, he's incorporated skills from these into his big wave approach, performing aerial spins and backflips on waves of 20 feet (6 meters) and more (opposite).

More recently, Jaws has served as a springboard for women's big-wave surfing to soar to its own lofty heights. For decades, Hawaiian stalwart Keala Kennelly has been leading the charge in the water and out, battling for equal representation and pay in big-wave competition. A victory came in November 2016, when a field of 12 descended on Jaws for the first-ever WSL Women's Big Wave event. Out in the lineup, they faced the same hectic high winds and giant waves as the men, but when local Paige Alms took out the win, she left with a far smaller paycheck. For Kennelly and her cohort, the event was a great step, but there was still much work to be done.

Following two more years of impassioned lobbying, the WSL finally capitulated and announced equal prize money going forward— becoming the first global sports league to do so. The women returned to Jaws soon after for what was undoubtedly a landmark event. It's clear, however, that the true impact will be felt by the next generation of young women, who can now dream of a career forged around the pursuit of big waves. Early dividends came in January 2021, when a historic swell bore down on the coast and more women than ever featured in the pack.

Among them were traditional battlers like Kennelly, Alms, and Andrea Moller, plus several fresher faces for whom they'd opened the door.

The session's defining moment featured French surfer Justine Dupont, who after descending a watery mountain, pulled up into the best barrel of the day. When she emerged through the mist with her hands raised high, amid the thunder of white water and the howls from the channel, you could just make out the sound of a glass ceiling being well and truly shattered. ⌒

The strong offshore winds that often accompany giant swells make paddling in a daunting prospect. When everything goes right, a vertical drop awaits, as demonstrated by Albee Layer (above). When it goes wrong, surfers become held in the lip as the wave falls away beneath them, sending them plunging several stories down into the trough, as demonstrated by Tom Dosland (opposite).

What You Need to Know

Level:
Only the most skilled big-wave surfers on earth should attempt to surf Jaws.

Best time to visit:
Giant swells with good winds are most likely between November and February.

What to bring:
Most opt for a 6-foot (1.8-meter) tow board or modern gun between 8 and 11 feet (2.4 and 3.3 meters) long.

What to do when it's flat:
Even if Jaws isn't working, the island has plenty more great surf spots, which work consistently throughout the winter months.

Fun fact:
The break was given the name Jaws by the first group to surf there in 1975, after a photo from the session showed the wave resembling the mouth of a shark.

The plus to surf:
i. South Shore of Oahu; ii. Big Island

NORTH PACIFIC OCEAN

HAWAII

PAPUA NEW GUINEA

TAHITI

Coral Sea

A Modern Upwelling in the Original Surf City

Waikiki, Hawaii,
United States

Located just outside Honolulu on Oahu's South Shore, Waikiki's fabled reefs are known as the birthplace of modern surfing. But in fact, their connection to wave-riding culture goes back considerably further.

According to historian Matt Warshaw, the stretch ranked second only to Kona on the Big Island as ancient Hawaii's most popular surfing area. From around 1200 onwards, royalty and commoners alike would strip off and paddle out to ride the gently spilling rollers on all manner of craft.

As was the case across the islands, surfing's popularity declined rapidly throughout the 19th century as missionaries arrived, decimating the population through disease, imposing long working hours, and discouraging what they deemed an immodest leisure pursuit. By the end of the century, Hawaii's rich wave-riding culture had been all but extinguished.

However, in the early 20th century, Waikiki would provide the stage for a grand revival. Led by young Hawaiians such as Duke Kahanamoku, the practice was encouraged by a new group of imperial overlords who saw surfing's power as a tool to draw in foreign tourists. Following numerous glowing features in the international press, by the 1920s the azure lineups were filled with skilled locals and floundering tourists. On the sand, a group of surf instructors-cum-tour guides known as the Waikiki Beach Boys established what would become the surfing lifestyle.

While Kahanamoku spread wave riding across the world in the ensuing decades, at home, Waikiki's mellow breaks began to shrink from the media limelight. By the early 1970s, longboarding had fallen out of fashion and the surf world's focus had shifted firmly to the waves on the island's North Shore. It would take another cultural sea change, on the other side of the millennium, for the sport's birthplace to regain its global influence.

In surf magazines' rush to unveil frightening new slabs and cutting-edge shredding, most had completely lost interest in the sort of easy peelers and smooth surfing to which the everyday wave rider most relates. It was only with the rise of online platforms and a proliferation of independent creators that enclaves flush with these qualities regained their prestige.

In Waikiki, this shift happened to coincide with the rise of a new generation of longboarding talent: a diverse crew of prodigious men and women, each with an effortless and highly watchable style. At the forefront were the likes of Kelis Kaleopa'a and Kaniela Stewart, who quickly got sponsored and began winning events, often beating out those more than 10 years their senior. The talent of these young guns was fostered, facilitated, and inspired by a well-respected crew of elders affectionately known as aunties and uncles. Some shaped their boards. Others taught them where to sit in the lineup. And all instilled in them an understanding of Waikiki's long surf history, ensuring that whenever they were chaired up the beach after a victory, they knew exactly on whose shoulders they really stood. ⌒

While Waikiki's city skyline looms high above the shoreline, the iconic Diamond Head dominates the vista to the south (previous spread, left). Keani Canullo blending power and flow on a board shaped by local luminary Kai Sallas (opposite). Nique Miller moved over from the U.S. mainland in her late teens and quickly fell in love with the waves and the diverse surf community who welcomed her with open arms (above).

Each patch of reef represents its own surf break. Featured here (above, from left to right) are Sandbar, Canoes, and Queens. Originally from Chicago, Haley Otto (opposite) is another mainlander who's become a celebrated member of the local logging scene with an approach inspired by Hawaiian icons like Honolua Blomfield and Kelia Moniz.

What You Need to Know

Level:
Waikiki hosts waves suited to everyone from total beginners to top-level rippers.

Best time to visit:
The prime window is from April to October, when long period swell are fanned by nonstop offshore trade winds.

What to bring:
A longboard and plenty of patience for navigating the always-crowded peaks.

What to do when it's flat:
Hike to the summit of Diamond Head.

Fun fact:
Stand-up surfing was captured on film for the first time in Waikiki in 1906.

The plus to surf:
i. North-West Maui; ii. Kauai

NORTH PACIFIC OCEAN

ii.

3

i.

HAWAII

PAPUA NEW GUINEA

TAHITI

Coral Sea

Ride Everything:

The Long and the Short

The surfboard is a simple tool with the capacity to bring immense joy. It can captivate surfers as much as the waves they seek. Over decades, changes in board design have altered our perceptions of surfing. Some elements of surfboards have changed dramatically since ancient cultures first took to the waves, yet some haven't changed at all.

BY JAMIE P. CURRIE

Members of the North Bondi Surf Life Saving Club, captured in 1948. The dominance of the surf life-saving movement in Australia at that time meant boards were large and cumbersome, built for paddling speed rather than wave-riding performance. However, when a group of American surfers arrived in 1956 with "Malibu" style boards, the Aussies quickly adopted the design.

Simple Treasures

Before the American novelist Herman Melville became famous for writing about people chasing whales, he wrote about people chasing waves. In his 1849 novel *Mardi: and a Voyage Thither*, based on Melville's travels in Tahiti and the Marquesas Islands, the narrator observes surfers on a fictitious South Seas island. He notes that surfboards were "held in high estimation; invariably oiled after use; and hung up conspicuously in the dwelling of the owner."

In 1891, after visiting the Hawaiian island of Niʻihau, American chemist and bibliographer of science, Henry Carrington Bolton, wrote that "wave-sliding boards" were "carefully smoothed ... frequently rubbed with coconut oil, and are pre-served with great solicitude, sometimes wrapped in cloths."

In Hawaii, these ancient and precious boards were known as olos, alaias, and paipos. They were made from the wood of wiliwili, koa, or breadfruit trees and then treated with nut oil. Olo boards were up to 20 feet (6 meters) long, incredibly heavy, and reserved for Hawaiian royalty only. Highly revered, these boards were created by skilled craftspeople and demanded rites and prayers.

Surfing may be known as the sport of royalty in ancient Polynesia, but it was also widely practiced by society: mothers and children and grandparents would be seen together on the waves. As in ancient Polynesia, around the world, wave-riding communities developed in most places where there was water. In 1834, James Alexander wrote of watching surfing in Accra, Ghana: "From the beach, meanwhile, might be seen boys swimming into the sea, with light boards under their stomachs. They waited for a surf; and then came rolling in like a cloud on the top of it." Historically, some surfed for fun, while others did so for transport or hunting. All around the world and throughout history, people have ridden crafts thoughtfully designed for local condi-tions and fashioned from local materials.

Surfboards have evolved considerably in the intervening centuries, but what remains is the →

→ pleasure they bring. A good surfboard is enchanting. To an owner, magic resides in the wood, fiberglass, or foam. It is imbued with the memories of waves ridden and trips taken. The heel dents, dings, and dirty wax tell tales of wondrous moments, never to be repeated. A surfboard may be a simple craft, but it holds a value far beyond the sum of its parts.

The Tail Wags the Dog

Surfboards remained long, heavy, wooden, and finless for many years, a design more or less true to the original Hawaiian boards that became known as the plank. American Tom Blake constructed lighter, hollow versions of the same basic model in the late 1920s, but despite surfing's growing popularity, boards were slow to evolve. Hollow boards and planks coexisted until the late 1940s with few changes except the types of wood used for construction.

Shapes began to change in the postwar era, thanks largely to the experimentation of American surfer Bob Simmons, who applied his mathematical and analytical talents to board design, introducing what we recognize today as rocker and foiled rails. He was also the first to trial foam and fiberglass rather than wood, materials that had been invented in the 1930s and developed during the war years.

Simmons died in a surfing accident in 1954, and it was left to other Californian boardmakers, Hobie Alter and Dave Sweet, to produce the first polyurethane boards in 1956. New materials were revolutionizing surfboard design and performance. Not only did boards become lighter and more maneuverable, but they were far easier to shape and mass-produce—thus bringing surfing to a wider audience.

Throughout the 1950s and 1960s, nearly all boards were longboards, measuring 10 feet (3 meters) and over. These boards were largely dictated by the surfing that people aspired to, an economy of movement directly descended from the Hawaiian nobility and the desire to dance on waves.

Then, in 1967, everything changed. The shortboard revolution altered the surfing landscape forever. It began in the earlier part of the decade with Californian George Greenough's short, stubby kneeboards. Though regarded today as an icon within surf lore, at the time, Greenough was considered something of an oddity, as were the boards he rode. When surfboards became 3 feet (1 meter)

shorter, Greenough looked like a prophet. First known as involvement surfing, because they enabled riders to get closer to the waves, the move to shortboards was perhaps the most impactful moment in surf history. It didn't just change what was under surfers' feet, it completely altered their perception of waves, allowing them to perform tighter turns, take steeper drops, and, eventually, find their way into the tube. There was no going back.

The shortboard revolution was a touchstone for the radical attitudes that defined surfing of this era. People wanted to go faster on their surfboards and further away from beach cultures that had become staid and crowded. Surfing moved on, and boards and styles that had been the epitome of cool at breaks like Malibu were set alight in its wake.

Through the 1970s, board design continued to evolve, as did surfing performance. The shorter shapes were a new realm, and if style had been the collateral damage of the shortboard revolution, Gerry Lopez reminded us that it still defined surfing at the highest level. His performances at Pipeline, on his iconic Lightning Bolt surfboards, are still the stuff of dreams: Lopez standing zen-like, with arms low and unflinching, emerging from a cavernous pit.

The nuances of shortboard design became more refined throughout the 1980s, but there was largely a period of calm after the storm of the revolution. Rockers, rails, and concaves were tweaked. Tail shapes morphed to square or squashed; rounded or pin; swallows, diamonds, or fish. The most significant developments were in fin design. Until the early '80s, surfboards always had a single fin. Twin fins existed sporadically before this, notably in the designs of Simmons and Greenough, but it wasn't until Australia's Mark Richards won four consecutive world titles from 1979 to 1982 on his own twin-fin designs that they rocketed to popularity. In 1981, the three-fin surfboard, known as the thruster, was pioneered by another Australian, Simon Anderson, closely followed by Glen Winton's quad fin designs in 1982.

Regressive Progression

The early 1990s brought a period of board design that benefited the most competent surfers to the same degree as it hindered everyone else. Surfboards varied in length between 6 and 7 feet (1.8 to 2.1 meters), but were almost exclusively thin, narrow, and highly rockered. Boards from this era are often

called potato chips, and during this time the average surfer may have surfed better on an actual chip. While good for the steep, fast, and hollow waves frequented by professionals, these designs were useless for casual surfers and worse than useless for beginners—yet, mercenary surf retailers sold them anyway.

The poster boy of this era was Kelly Slater. What many don't realize is that Slater is 5 feet 9 inches (1.75 meters) and around 160 pounds (72.5 kilos), with a degree of paddle-fitness and athleticism that was off the charts and a level of skill never before seen. For most of us, jumping on a board like Slater's would be akin to taking a Formula One car grocery shopping, and then trying to navigate it around the aisles.

Cutting Back

There's a fundamental law of nature that states things tend to move in circles. The same is true of design trends. Eventually, we cycle back, wondering what we might have missed. Sometime in the late 1990s and early 2000s, surfers began to take a retrospective look at boards.

Just as potato-chip designs were instigated by high-profile surfers, so too was the move back to retro designs and their evolution into the more user-friendly shapes we see in lineups today. The most high-profile example of this was Tom Curren, the surfer with the most universally lauded style in history. Curren's embrace of alternative designs, most notably the fish shape, paved the way for surfing's return to fun and accessibility. Freesurfers like Dave Rastovich and Rob Machado also embraced alternative boards and furthered this movement.

Today there is a diverse range of craft in every lineup, thanks to the popularity of YouTubers like Jamie O'Brien showing that foam boards designed for beginners can also be fun in the heaviest lineup in the world, fellow Hawaiian Mason Ho, who makes any board on any wave look like the most fun you could have—or George Greenough, who you'll find catching waves on a surf mat.

The Magic Board

The surfboard is a curious tool. On the surface, it's low-tech and strikingly simple, yet what lies beneath remains mysterious. No one can really tell you →

The surfboard is a curious tool. On the surface, it's low-tech and strikingly simple, yet what lies beneath remains mysterious. No one can really tell you what the perfect surfboard is.

→ what the perfect surfboard is. There are designs better suited to certain waves, but there is no one size that fits all. Beyond this, there are still intricacies in the manufacturing process that mean no two surfboards are identical. Despite computer-aided design and machine shaping, most surfboards still require an element of hands-on input. A machine might cut the basic foam blank, but it's up to people to glass and sand it. It's in these latter finishing processes that magic or disaster might happen.

These inconsistencies in manufacturing and ever-evolving theories of design mean the concept of the "magic board" persists. Based on instinct rather than any sort of empirical evidence, it's an alchemy that most surfers can't explain or predict—they just know when a board feels right.

Ride Everything

Board design today is more inclusive than ever before. There's a craft for every sea state, and the only limiting factor is your imagination. Beyond "traditional" surfboards of all shapes and sizes, there are finless boards, surfmats, handplanes, bellyboards, SUPs, foils, skimboards, bodyboards, and things that don't look like surfboards at all. But regardless of your personal aesthetic, the aim remains much the same.

We might sum up the decades of board design by thinking about the definitive styles of the eras. We went from gliding and trimming, to cutbacks and carves, to ripping, shredding, and hacking. Today, we do it all. Surfing doesn't always need to be about how radical your turns are or how fast you go. What matters is that you're out there.

For many people, the emphasis is simply being in the water. In that way, you might say that surfing has returned to its roots. As surf historian Matt Warshaw notes in the final chapter of his epic *The History of Surfing*, despite all that has changed, from one perspective "the sport remains very much unchanged. All those women and silver-haired seniors now in the lineup—that's a throwback to ancient times." ~

Agony and Ecstasy

Teahupoo, Tahiti,
French Polynesia

No wave inspires more fear and awe than the mighty Teahupoo. Located off the southern tip of Tahiti, its name translates as "the hall of cracked skulls"—an epithet that tells you all you need to know about the risks of surfing there. The spot's uniquely square tubes are largely the result of the steep angle of the reef below. Arriving from deep water, swells are stopped suddenly in their tracks, as hundreds of tons of Pacific lift, lurch forward, and fall like a sledgehammer onto the waist-deep coral.

Equally critical to the development of Teahupoo's legend is the deepwater channel that snakes alongside it. By granting relatively safe passage for watercraft, it allows camera people to get close enough to feel the spit. Plus, it offers a side-on vantage, looking straight into the wave's maw, creating images that convey the intensity of the tube in a way a land angle never could.

It's from this hallowed patch of ocean that many of modern surfing's most iconic moments have been captured. Among the most poignant was Laird Hamilton's Millennium Wave, a tow-in so exhilarating it reduced the Hawaiian strongman to tears in the channel straight afterward. When the footage was released to the world, it fired a starting gun on decades of relentless big wave slab exploration.

Another was Keala Kennelly's 2016 ride—achieved just a few years after she had her face sliced open by the reef—for which she became the first woman ever to win the "Barrel of the Year" big wave award.

Recently a young generation of Tahitians has taken the reins at Teahupoo, aided by a series of pandemic travel bans that relieved them of the need to battle the world's best for every set wave on classic days. Now, when a giant swell rolls in, scores of locals can be found paddling into barrels of a similar magnitude to Hamilton's Millennium tow effort—many of whom were only just born when it happened. You could say things have come full circle, but to observe their talents, it seems the story of progression at the break is nowhere near over. ⌁

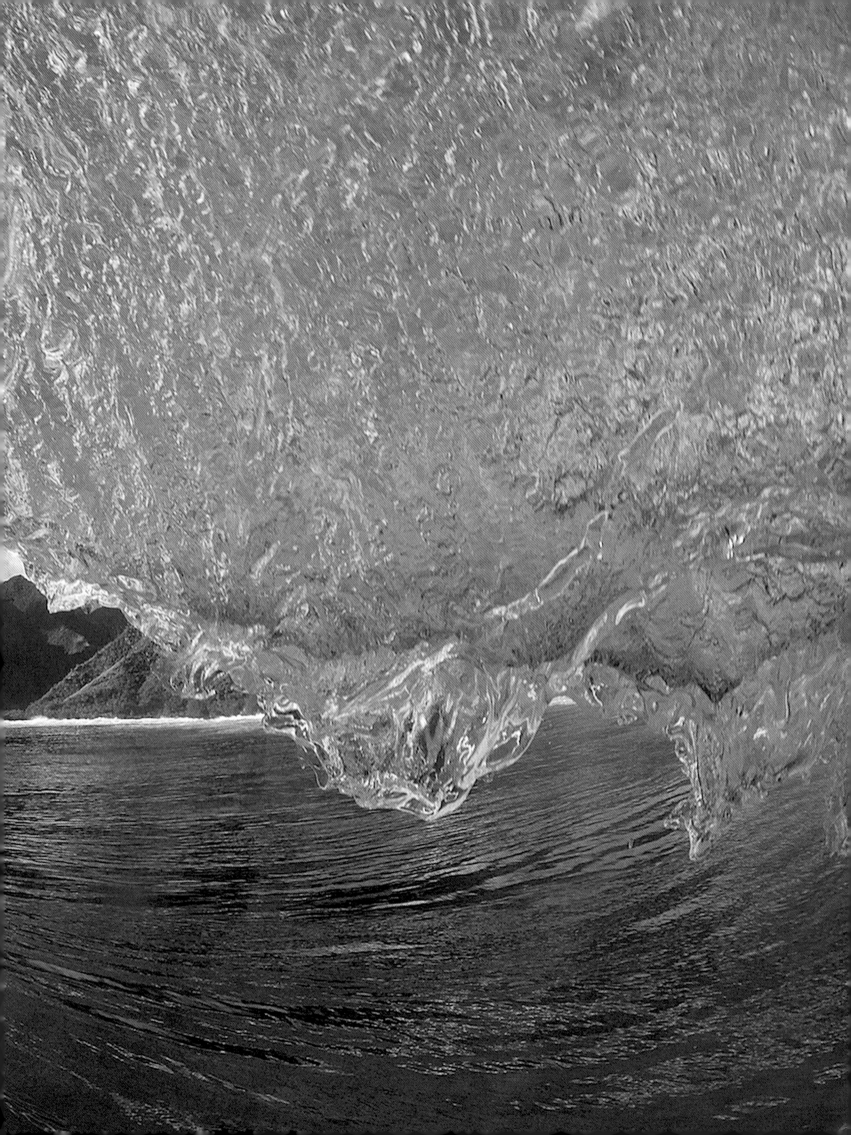

Perennial fixture Raimana Van Bastolaer locked into the belly of the beast (opening spread, right). When a giant set approaches, surfers are forced to scramble to get over it. The nightmare they're trying to avoid frequently becomes manifest, as stragglers are dragged backwards over the falls into the maelstrom below (below). Shane Dorian, clinging on through a soupy west bowl (opposite).

What You Need to Know

Level:
Advanced surfers can manage head-high days at the spot, but anything bigger than that is expert only.

Best time to visit:
Peak swell season is between April and October.

What to bring:
A pintail and a Gath helmet.

What to do when it's flat:
Hike in the mountains, go snorkeling, or just laze under a palm tree.

Fun fact:
First ridden by Tahitians, the wave was publicly pioneered at size by professional bodyboarders Mike Stewart and Ben Severson in the late 1980s.

The plus to surf:
i. Moorea; ii. Raiatea

PAPUA NEW GUINEA

Coral Sea

ii. ≋   i. ≋   TAHITI
4 ≋

SOUTH PACIFIC OCEAN

Tasman Sea

NEW ZEALAND

Tradition Reimagined in Papua New Guinea

Papua New Guinea

Nestled in the northwest corner of Melanesia, Papua New Guinea is famed for its tapestry of ancient cultures and rich biodiversity. Just offshore, you'll find an equally varied range of tropical breaks, frequented by a surf community steeped in tradition.

Pinwheeling points, expansive beaches, and high-quality reefs dot the mainland and a string of outer isles. For as long as anyone can remember, many have been ridden by locals on *palangs,* wooden boards hand carved from vast tree trunks. More recently, following an influx of fiberglass boards left by visitors, local surfers have sought to reimagine

their ancestors' craft. In Tupira, a group has established a shaping bay, where they build modern boards from abundant local balsa. Over the course of a decade, their efforts have not only succeeded in preserving the island's surfing heritage and relieving locals' reliance on donations but also in creating what is surely the world's shortest and most sustainable surfboard supply chain.

Their outfit is not the only enterprising way the country has managed the advent of surf tourism. In 1989, the Surf Association of Papua New Guinea established a unique scheme that hands stewardship of each break to the local community who live adjacent to it. Visitors pay a small fee to surf and their numbers are controlled through quotas. At the end of the season, each village spends the money collected on community projects, such as improved water sanitation or a new school building.

While some might balk at the idea of a pay-to-surf policy, here it allows communities to benefit directly from surf tourism, while staving off the prospect of the dangerous overcrowding that blights other tropical destinations. Against a backdrop of widespread environmental destruction from mining and illegal logging, the scheme gives Indigenous communities a way to draw financial benefit from protecting their coastlines. Beyond its impact within Papua New Guinea, it is hoped its success will inspire other emerging surf destinations across the South Pacific. ∼

The town of Wewak is home to a small community of passionate local surfers (opposite) and a series of quality points and reef breaks, ranging from the soft and cruisey to fast and tubular (above). Visiting Italian surfer Leo Fioravanti flies high above the palms (below).

As the crew paddled out from the boat at a remote patch of reef, children from the local village rushed onto a huge bit of driftwood to watch the show. Each time a surfer took off, they erupted into a cacophony of hoots and laughter. "It was pure and refreshing to witness the kids' curiosity and genuine stoke," recalled photographer Ryan Craig in *Surfer* magazine (above).

What You Need to Know

Level:
Beginner to expert.

Best time to visit:
The prime window from November to April sees consistent swells ranging from waist high to overhead.

What to bring:
A UPF rashie to keep the sun off while shredding.

What to do when it's flat:
Attend a "sing-sing," a gathering of tribe members in traditional dress performing their ancestral dances and songs.

Fun fact:
In 2017, the country held its first international surfing event, the Kumul World Longboard Championships, in Tupira.

The plus to surf:
i. New Georgia, Solomon Islands; ii. Kavieng, New Ireland

PHILIPPINES

PHILIPPINE SEA

NORTH PACIFIC OCEAN

INDONESIA

SINGAPORE

PAPUA NEW GUINEA

Arafura Sea

Coral Sea

AUSTRALIA

Great Australian Bight

NEW ZEALAND

New Zealand's Perfect Peninsula

Coromandel Peninsula,
New Zealand

Widely regarded as one of the most beautiful countries on earth due to a sparse population and varied, dramatic geography, from a surfer's perspective New Zealand is paradise.

The Coromandel Peninsula juts out from the northeast corner of the country's North Island. The peninsula is narrow—only 25 miles (40 kilometers) wide at its widest point—and the majority of the population lives in coastal areas. It has a mountainous spine that runs along the interior and is dominated by forest. Despite being close to Auckland, it retains a feeling of rugged remoteness.

The west coast faces the sheltered Hauraki Gulf, but the many bays and beaches of the east coast are exposed to South Pacific swells. Because of its proximity to Auckland, the Coromandel area has been surfed since the 1950s. Even so, due to the sheer number and variety of spots, it's still possible to find quiet waves today.

This coast has a high density of quality surf spots, from reefs and points to superb beach breaks. One of the best in the area is Whangamata, in the town of the same name. This predominantly left-breaking wave, known as The Bar, is created by sediment deposited at the mouth of the Otahu River. Surf legend Gerry Lopez has described this wave as "the jewel of the Pacific" and when it's on, it provides hollow sections and long, rippable walls. Just along from here, at the main beach in Whangamata, you'll find a variety of left and right peaks. As Coromandel spots go, these might be busier than most.

The Coromandel Peninsula is littered with beautiful beach-break setups. Another beach in the area offering geological interest to accompany quality waves is Hot Water Beach. A popular vacation beach due to the hot water springs on the shore, there can also be hollow and fun waves offshore. Some others of note are Te Karo Bay, Tairua, Pauanui, and Kuaotunu beaches. All of these spots offer left and right peaks that are accessible to a wide range of surfers and craft. ~

The forerunners of a cyclone swell arrive with pristine conditions (previous spread, left). Asher Pacey and Jason Salisbury head for the coast, armed with a few ears of corn and various surf craft (previous spread, right). A pumping day in Whangamata (above). Matt Hewitt sits deep in the pit (below). Dylan Goodale engages his rail (opposite).

When it comes to mythic local legends and underground chargers, New Zealand's surf community is supremely well endowed. Here, the enigmatic Rangi Ormond typifies the trope (below). Located on the peninsula's northeastern edge, the Orua coastline features a cornucopia of awe-inspiring coastal geography, including some of the country's largest sea caves (opposite).

What You Need to Know

Level:
Beginner to expert.

Best time to visit:
May to September for waves, December to March for warmth.

What to bring:
A good, solid rental car, ideally a 4 × 4.

What to do when it's flat:
Dig your own hot water pool on Hot Water Beach, or visit the Lost Spring. Then relax and wait for the swell to fill in.

Local tip:
Don't get lost in the woods.

The plus to surf:
i. Taranaki; ii. Gisborne

The Best of the Wild Wild West

Margaret River,
Australia

Despite its prime Indian Ocean frontage, the waves in Western Australia's capital of Perth are really nothing to write home about. But drive three hours south to Margaret River and you'll find some of the finest breaks in the whole of the country.

Following the word of city surfers who visited in the 1950s, wave-riding communities slowly began to sprout among Margie's bucolic patchwork of farms, vineyards, and eucalyptus forests. In the decades since, each has evolved into its own enclave filled with top-level pros, underground chargers, and workaday grafters, many of whom earn their crust from the ocean only to spend their leisure time being humbled by it.

Throughout the winter, the region's dozen or so named breaks are battered by waves from the roaring forties, with each sweeping line of swell ending its journey on a variety of shallow limestone ledges and hard-packed sand. Almost all demand a high level of skill, athleticism, and a solid dose of fortitude.

The most famous is the Margaret River Main Break—an A-frame peak with long tapering walls →

→ that can hold up to 16 feet (5 meters). The final section ends on a nasty rock shelf known as the Surgeon's Table—just one of many ominously-named features of the region's ocean topography.

By the early 1970s, the spot was well attended by a crew of hardened surfers who would tackle the waves on heavy leashless single fins. Among them was Ian "Kanga" Cairns, and it was only thanks to the audacity imbued by his experiences there that he was able to so confidently attack the North Shore later in the decade, taking the world by storm at Sunset Beach and beyond. His was a central role in the infamous Bustin' Down the Door years,

a period of intense competition and progression, the effects of which would reverberate through global surf culture for decades to come.

Cairns also had a crack at a wave known as The Box in the early 1980s—a short, sharp, and obscenely shaped slab that breaks just over from Main Break. But most credit local bodyboarders with properly setting the bar out there in the decade following. Chief in that pack was Ryan Hardy, son of another 70s Main Break standout, and one part of a sprawling local surf dynasty. His brother Gene is also a waterman par excellence, thought to be the only wave rider on earth to

land himself on the cover of both a major surf and a major bodyboard magazine. Along with his wife Sunny, he's raising the next generation of hard-charging Hardys in the form of his young daughter Willow, who at just 15 is already one of Australia's most exciting up-and-comers.

While most of her contemporaries on the junior tour will have already traveled extensively, Hardy has honed her talents exclusively in her home state. And, like Cairns half a century before her, the wild waves around Margie's seem to have set her up pretty well. With good surf almost every day, why would you want to live anywhere else? ~

Fifteen-year-old Willow Hardy drops into a slabbing left (previous spread, right). Margaret River local Jack Robinson has become Australia's top-rated male surfer in recent years. Here, he casually navigates a yawning cavern at The Box (top, left). Felicity Palmateer and Mia McCarthy hike in Boranup Forest (top, right). Local shaper Matt Percy with his quiver of unique bonzer creations (bottom, left).

Felicity Palmateer and Mia McCarthy setting up camp (above). Margies Main Break in the rearview mirror (below). After a childhood spent surfing with his dad, legendary local shaper Matt Manners, Shaun Manners has developed into one of the region's most explosive freesurfers with an incredible ability on rail, in the barrel, and flying high above the lip (opposite).

What You Need to Know

Level:
Intermediate to expert.

Best time to visit:
There are waves year-round. Winter (June to August) sees the biggest swells, while fall (March to May) is most likely to welcome clean conditions, making it most surfers' favorite season.

What to bring:
Locals favor thick pintails around 7 feet (2 meters) in length, with hard rails for plenty of hold.

What to do when it's flat:
Explore the magnificent Margaret River caves or visit one of the world-famous wineries.

Local tip:
Start your surf check at the Surfers Point parking lot, which offers views over half a dozen breaks, including Main Break, and will likely be full of locals who may share a tip on where to check next.

The plus to surf:
i. North West Coast; ii. Albany

Nature's Nastiest Staircase

Shipstern Bluff,
Australia

In the far southeast corner of the Tasman Peninsula, beneath a towering stern-shaped bluff, a series of boulder-strewn plateaus descend like a staircase into the seething ocean below. Just a few meters out from the base, you'll find a wave so malformed that most wouldn't deign to call it a surf spot at all.

It's exactly because of its many mutations that Shipstern Bluff—known locally as Shippies—has become one of the most iconic big waves on earth. Its "steps" as they're known, are a sequence of ledges that emerge sporadically throughout a ride, frequently sending surfers airborne and cartwheeling into the trough.

Despite conflicting tales of who exactly saw and surfed the wave first, most agree it was pioneered by a Tassie guru named Andy Campbell in the late 1990s. For years, he'd make the long two-hour hike through the dense bush and spend an afternoon packing lonely tubes purely for the thrill of it, with no cameras or jet skis in sight. Around the turn of the millennium, Campbell invited a few Aussie pros to join him, and in 2001, the wave was unveiled to the world via a photo splash in Tracks magazine. Among the crew on that trip was Hawaiian charger Kieren Perrow, whose baptism of fire began by splitting his lip while jumping in off the rocks. "Not ideal," he recalled, "given how sharky the place is." However, things improved quickly from there, and the photos of the session sent heads spinning across the surfing world.

While Campbell moved away, eventually trading his board and backpack for a camera and bulletproof vest in Syria, other locals were ruling the spot by the end of the decade, most, like their predecessor, working day jobs and charging for the love of it. According to photographer Stu Gibson, hospital orderly Mikey Brennan has been a perennial standout—not only for his incredible tube riding but his playful mastery of the wave's scariest feature, busting rail grabs and 360° spins during periods of forced mid-wave flight. ～

Local charger Mikey Brennan navigating a gurgling set of Shipstern steps (previous spread). A section of the ship-shaped bluff overlooking the wave recently collapsed, leaving the rock platform below strewn with scree and giant boulders, adding further peril to an already tricky entry into the lineup (above). Top Aussie slab wrangler Laura Enever in the tube (below).

What You Need to Know

Level:
Suitable for big-wave hellmen and women only.

Best time to visit:
The biggest swells thunder in from April to October.

What to bring:
Since the water temp hovers around 53 °F (12 °C) in the prime winter months, you'll need a 5/3 mm wetsuit and boots, plus a hood and gloves on particularly chilly days.

What to do when it's flat:
Check out some of the other waves around the neighbouring islands, or get adventurous and try the bushwalks that have made Tasmania famous.

Local tip:
In summer, keep your eyes peeled for snakes on the track into Shippies, and remember to pack water for the walk in.

The plus to surf:
i. North Coast of Tasmania; ii. East Coast of Tasmania

MALAYSIA

INDONESIA

SINGAPORE

PAPUA NEW GUINEA

Arafura Sea

Coral Sea

TAHITI

AUSTRALIA

INDIAN OCEAN

Great Australian Bight

i.

ii.

Tasman Sea

8

NEW ZEALAND

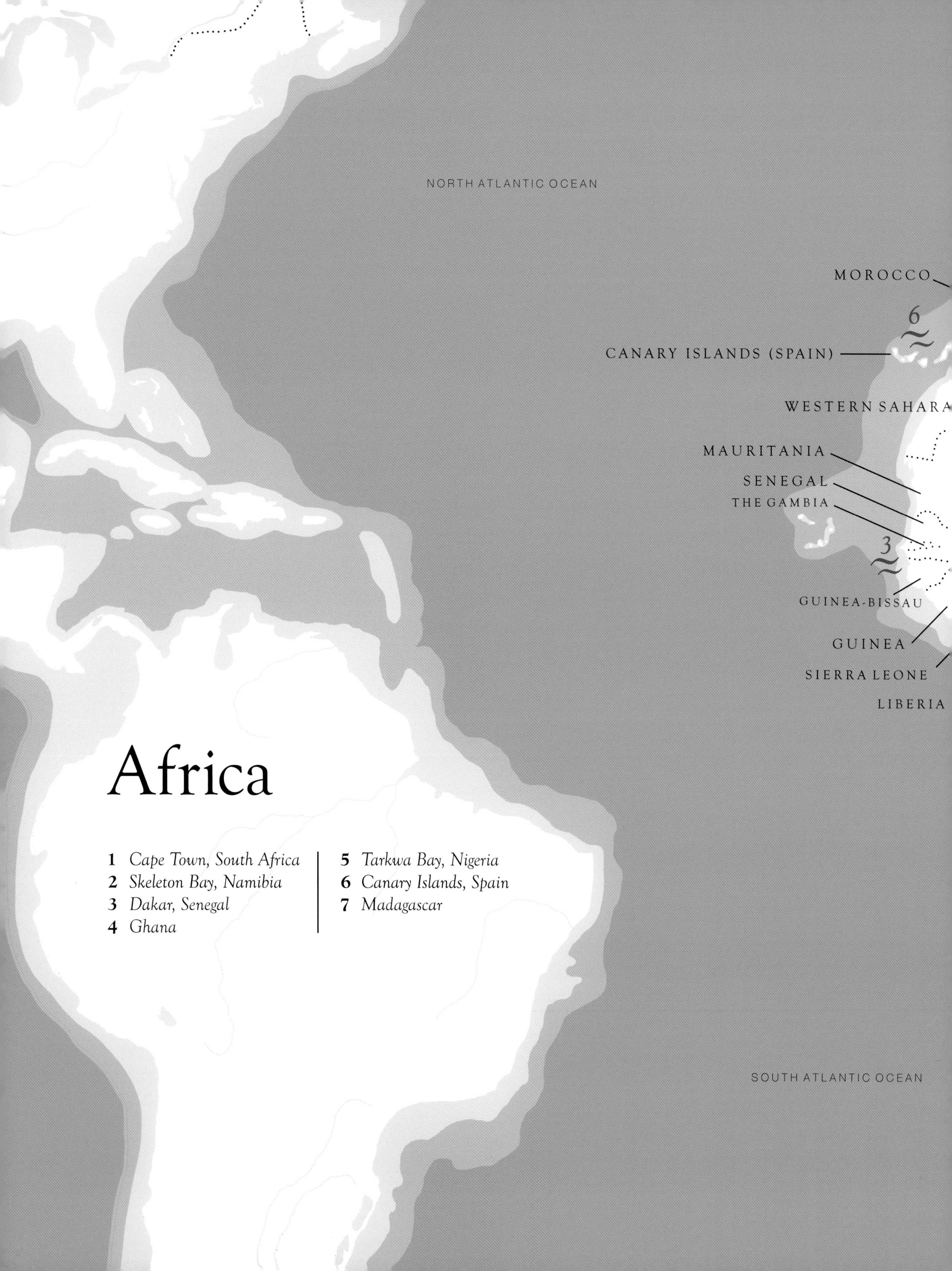
NORTH ATLANTIC OCEAN
MOROCCO
6
CANARY ISLANDS (SPAIN)
WESTERN SAHARA
MAURITANIA
SENEGAL
THE GAMBIA
3
GUINEA-BISSAU
GUINEA
SIERRA LEONE
LIBERIA
SOUTH ATLANTIC OCEAN

Africa

1 *Cape Town, South Africa*
2 *Skeleton Bay, Namibia*
3 *Dakar, Senegal*
4 *Ghana*
5 *Tarkwa Bay, Nigeria*
6 *Canary Islands, Spain*
7 *Madagascar*

Tubes at the Tip of Africa

*Cape Town,
South Africa*

One of South Africa's three capital cities, Cape Town is the oldest city in the country and the second largest next to Johannesburg. Here, at the very tip of Africa, dramatic mountain peaks tower over a bustling, cosmopolitan city that spills onto white sand beaches. From a surfer's perspective, Cape Town has something to offer everyone. There is a huge variety of waves for all levels of surfer in close proximity, from mellow beach breaks for beginners or longboards, to epic barrels and world-renowned big-wave spots like Dungeons.

The prominence of the Cape Peninsula means there's a huge swell window, and this in turn means you'll be able to find a rideable wave on any day of the year. Furthermore, it's likely you'll find a spot that's offshore.

The best bet is to head south of Cape Town itself. A wave known as The Wedge is the closest spot to the city and breaks near the harbor wall, but there are far better spots just a short distance away. Muizenberg (also known as Surfer's Corner) is one of the most recognized but also most accessible spots in the area. It's situated on the east side of the Cape and has multiple peaks good for all levels. Directly opposite this on the west side, there's a concentration of spots including The Hoek, Dunes, and Long Beach. These spots offer everything from world-class A-frame beach break tubes to more mellow waves suitable for beginners.

Whenever surfing focuses on South Africa it tends to center around J-Bay and Cape St. Francis. Perhaps rightly so, as two of the world's most iconic point breaks—but that leaves some of the waves around the Cape to fly under the radar of traveling surfers. As with any peninsula, the best thing to do is take a drive. You never know what you might find.

The water temperature around the Cape Peninsula doesn't change much from season to season. Although it's not cold enough to be considered a cold-water location, you will need to wear a wetsuit as the water temperature remains consistent and chilly at 57–61 °F (14–16 °C). ⌁

After cutting his teeth around South Africa, Grant "Twiggy" Baker became one of the most accomplished big-wave surfers on earth, claiming victories at Mavericks, Nazaré, and Puerto Escondido. However, Dungeons remains one of his favorite stomping grounds (opposite). Jarrad Howse stands tall in a crystal cavern (above). Mikey February walks on the beach just down the road from Kommetjie, where he grew up (below).

The view looking north along Long Beach, past the surf breaks of Crons and Dunes to the cloud-shrouded Chapman's Peak and Table Moutain (previous spread). Grant "Twiggy" Baker surfs a rare big-wave reef half a mile out past Dungeons. Captured in 2008, this wave measured a whopping 61 feet (18.5 meters) making it still to this day the biggest ever ridden in South Africa (above).

What You Need to Know

Level:
Beginner to expert.

Best time to visit:
The spots around Cape Town will work at any time of year. Winter brings more swell, but southeast trade winds in summer mean that many spots on the west of the Cape Peninsula will be clean and offshore.

What to bring:
A good 4/3 wetsuit.

What to do when it's flat:
Hike the iconic Table Mountain. Go kitesurfing or windsurfing. The Cape Peninsula is well known for windy summers and offers world-class conditions for wind-powered board sports.

Local tip:
Get a 4 × 4 vehicle to access some of the more offbeat spots.

The plus to surf:
i. Durban; ii. St. Francis Bay

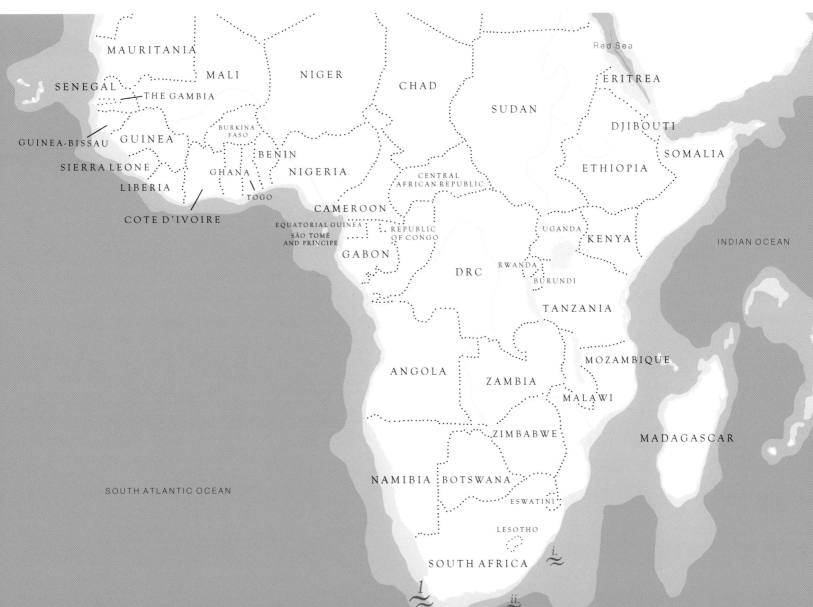

Racing Widow-Makers on the Skeleton Coast

Skeleton Bay,
Namibia

From high above, Pelican Point resembles a hooked finger, reaching out to protect the city of Walvis Bay from the brunt of the Atlantic. Move in closer and the body of the spit reveals filaments of dark emerald and red swirling into the yellow sands as if spilled from a paint can. Zoom in once more, to where the land meets the murky green ocean, and you'll see swell lines grinding down its gently curved edge.

That's the bit that caught Brian Gable's eye as he scrolled through satellite images of the region one day in 2008. He could tell the waves were long. But, from this digital vantage, there was no way he could have known he'd just stumbled across one of the best surf breaks on earth: a sand-bottom barrel so long and perfect, it would soon become the one by which all others were measured.

Gable, an IT specialist from California, was on the hunt for his entry to *Surfer Magazine*'s annual Google Earth Challenge—in which readers were →

→ invited to scour the world for potential new discoveries from the comfort of their armchairs. The magazine staff saw the potential of his find immediately, quickly announcing it as that year's winner. Soon after, footage of pro surfer Cory Lopez riding the wave now called Skeleton Bay sent shockwaves through the surfing world. Before long, the globe's top barrel jockeys were making regular pilgrimages and flooding the internet with mind-melting GoPro clips featuring the view from inside the 1.25-mile (2-kilometer) long tubes.

As it turned out, the wave had been surfed by Namibian locals prior to its grand unveiling, but rarely at the size and ferocity seen from 2008 onwards. Far from being a long-held secret, satellite imagery suggests the sandbar only took shape around the turn of the millennium, acquiring the nuances that make the wave world-class even more recently than that. Photographer Alan van Gysen once witnessed the shape of the shoreline change completely over the course of a single day, proving the spot remains as dynamic as ever.

While this has led some surfers to worry that the sandbar may soon straighten out and transform the wave into an unmakeable closeout, others disagree. To observe the cavalcade that descends every time a rare 6-foot (2-meter) swell lines up suggests that, in the face of this uncertainty, surfers have resolved to seize the day; to treat every whomping Skeleton Bay drainer as if it could be their last, and to combat the threat of fast-moving sand by planting feet, 4 × 4s, and broken boards firmly in it. ∼

The Skeleton Coast is defined by searing heat and huge rolling sand dunes, usually shrouded in dense ocean fog. Namibian bushmen refer to the region as "the land God made in anger" (previous spread). On every swell, a board graveyard can be found quickly accumulating on the point (top, left). Hawaiian Alex Smith takes in the view he traveled halfway across the world for (bottom, left).

Skeleton Bay specialist Benji Brand lines up for a barrel, with a GoPro camera in his mouth ready to record the ride (above). The swell direction and the precise curvature of the sandy shoreline together dictate the speed of the wave and the formation of the tube. Here, a perfectly angled swell meets a perfectly angled coast (below).

What You Need to Know

Level:
With marathon paddles, near-impossible airdrops, and incredibly fast and tricky tube sections, Skeleton Bay is expert only.

Best time to visit:
The wave is very fickle and only works a handful of times throughout the prime swell season: April to September.

What to bring:
All the surf equipment you need, plus plenty of food and water for refueling on the runaround.

What to do when it's flat:
The spit and lagoon are amazing for watching wildlife including seals, jackals, flamingoes, pelicans, and more.

Local tip:
The only building on the point is a lighthouse-cum-hotel called Pelican Point Lodge—five stars with prices to match. Most visitors travel in from Walvis Bay, a 30-minute drive in a 4 × 4.

The plus to surf:
i. North Skeleton Coast; ii. Luanda Area, Angola

West Africa's Surfing Stronghold

*Dakar,
Senegal*

Built on political stability, a culture that values art and sport in equal measure, and numerous top-quality breaks, the surf scene in Dakar, Senegal, has become a shining beacon of achievability in a region of abundant potential. Just outside the city, neighborhoods brim with surf schools, camps, and restaurants run by local shredders who've made their lives and livelihoods by the coast.

Some of the best-known breaks are on N'Gor Island, which sits a short boat ride from the town of N'Gor. Waves wrap around a pair of volcanic rock points located at either end. The right is particularly famous thanks to its appearance in Bruce Brown's surf documentary *The Endless Summer*, released in the mid-60s. Although N'Gor Island has developed significantly since, the narrow sandy streets, lack of vehicles, and patchwork of laid-back restaurants and art stores have ensured it remains a world away from the frenetic city life just across the channel.

Along the coast from N'Gor, the Almadies Peninsula juts out into the Atlantic like the bulge of a puzzle piece, marking mainland Africa's westernmost tip. Here a multitude of quality reefs swirls up swells from both hemispheres. Most notable on the north coast are the speedy lefts of Gauche de Loic. On the south, the now ironically named Secret Spot is the coast's best-known break, offering powerful lefts and rights in front of a beachside eatery that serves as a local hangout.

Just south of Les Almadies is Ouakam, arguably the region's best reef break. Backed by a towering and ornate city mosque, it offers world-class barrels on its day, breaking both left and right (top, left). A local surfer checks the waves at Secret Spot (top, right). Fishing boats line the shoreline in front of N'Gor village (bottom, right). Karim Diouf and Demba Gueye share a wave at Vivier Left (opposite).

A few doors down, the scene's most influential figure, Oumar Seye, runs a surf shop and restaurant, complete with a pool cut into the rocky shoreline where he played as a child. At a time when surfing was still considered a distraction from real work, Seye broke ground, becoming the country's first professional and standing as an inarguable demonstration of how the sport could pave a pathway to success. He's spent the last few decades mentoring the next generation, including Cherif Fall, who has developed into one of the continent's finest surfers, with international sponsorships and a place on the World Qualifying Series. He too has become a prominent local trendsetter, with shades of his unmistakably explosive and elastic style visible in the country's many promising up-and-comers.

Another local surfer representing Senegal on the global stage is Khadjou Sambe. When she first paddled out, aged 14, women were still a very rare sight in the lineup, but now her profile has ensured that's a thing of the past. In 2018, she seized an offer to fly to Santa Cruz to train with the organization Black Girls Surf. It was her first time leaving the country, and despite having no money and little English, she threw herself in with full determination. When she returned to Dakar, she co-founded a surf school with the organization on her local beach. Its goal is not only to teach Senegalese girls to surf but to "inspire them to be whatever they want"—a byproduct that is perhaps surf culture's finest legacy of all. ～

In 2021, 16-year-old Cherif Diop was awarded an International Surf Association Scholarship, providing funds for his education, surf equipment, and contest entry fees (above). In recent years, a concerted effort to welcome more local women and girls into the water seems to be paying off. Here, young ripper Déguéne Thiouna shows the new recruits how it's done at Secret Spot (opposite).

What You Need to Know

Level:
Intermediate to expert.

Best time to visit:
October to April sees swells arriving from both the north and south, meaning they'll usually be somewhere working, at least until the wind gets up.

What to bring:
Consider bringing booties for the urchin-covered reefs. Or, if you're feeling brave, just some tweezers to pull the spines out.

What to do when it's flat:
Visit some of the city's historic museums and art galleries, or the arts complex Villages des Arts for contemporary sculpture and modern art.

Local tip:
When surfing N'Gor Island right, watch out for "mami" and "papi," two rocks that pop up just in front of the takeoff.

The plus to surf:
i. Northwest Liberia; ii. Abidjan, Ivory Coast

Sampling Ghana's Rhythm and Groove

Ghana

Sitting at the center of the earth, just above zero latitude and longitude, Ghana has developed into a vibrant pocket of equatorial surf culture.

As Kevin Dawson outlines in the ground-breaking 2021 book *AFROSURF*, contrary to popular claims, riding waves is nothing new here. Drawing on accounts that date back hundreds of years, Dawson describes an ancient culture where bodysurfing and racing atop the breakers on canoes and boards were commonplace. Along a coastline with few natural harbors, these practices proved critical for fisherfolk navigating the surf in swell-battered coastal towns.

In 2019, just a year after he became the first Black African surfer from South Africa to qualify for the Championship Tour, Mikey February seized a window between events to visit one such place. Born and raised in South Africa, February enjoyed a meteoric rise in his early 20s, drawing global adoration for his supremely flowing style. Growing up, his parents were both professional creatives, passing on a passion for music, art, and aesthetics →

→ that permeates his approach in and out of the water. When February got the chance to travel to Ghana, following rumors of a beautiful sand-bottomed point and a lively local music scene, his goal was to combine these elements in a film project. He spent two weeks in a remote coastal town, with photographer Alan van Gysen and filmmakers Sam Smith and Wade Carroll, hanging out with fisherfolk, meeting musicians, and sharing waves with a few local surfers. The resulting short, entitled Nü RYTHMO, marked a refreshing divergence from the fruits of most surf media trips.

"We wanted to go there and get that wave," February explains, "but also, growing up in South Africa, I noticed the way people end up doing their surf edits, where they always show little pieces [of the culture] but it never really gives the people a voice or an in-depth feel of everything around. Essentially those are the people that make your trip so special, and so our plan was to try and capture that experience."

With the electrifying rhythms of live-recorded afrobeat mixed with the ambient chants of fisher-folk, the thrum of a concert crowd, and the crash of waves, the soundtrack truly succeeds in taking you there. On-screen, footage of locals launching boats and cavorting in mesmeric dance are interspersed with February's rides; waves finely threaded with the same rhythm and finesse. It's a vivid depiction of the deep links between surfing and dance that animate many of Ghana's emerging communities and a distinct approach to wave riding blooming right across the continent.

"We live mostly in a 'Western world' where so often we are trying to be like each other—especially in surfing," February writes in AFROSURF. "And we think that modern Western culture is always going to be the main influence. But if anything, I feel like African surf communities are going to be the ones to influence a lot of people around the rest of the world instead. It's a very exciting time." ~

A palm tree offers a welcome patch of shade for a pair of locals hard at work, while in the distance, February spies an oasis of his own (previous spread, right). Ghanaian musician Stevo Atambire is a master of the kologo, a two-stringed cousin of the banjo. Here, he performs live on the beach for the soundtrack and the opening sequence of Nü RYTHMO (opposite).

The fast and fickle nature of the town's most exposed section of beach means perfect waves frequently run off without a rider (above). Down the coast, in the lee of the point, the town's fishing fleet hauls their boats in through the shore break (below). Mikey February, frozen in a moment of signature style and poise as he hangs in the pocket of a right-hand reeler (opposite).

What You Need to Know

Level:
Beginner to expert.

Best time to visit:
May to October (the rainy season), when consistent swells arrive accompanied by morning offshores.

What to bring:
Wax is hard to get hold of in Ghana, so bring plenty and leave some behind if you can.

What to do when it's flat:
Dance the night away in the surf capital of Busua or explore the rainforest in Kakum National Park.

Local tip:
Brett Davies at Mr Brights Surf School has been instrumental in the development of the local surf scene. If you're looking to plan a trip, a chat with him is a great place to start.

The plus to surf:
i. Lomé Area, Togo; ii. Cotonou Area, Benin

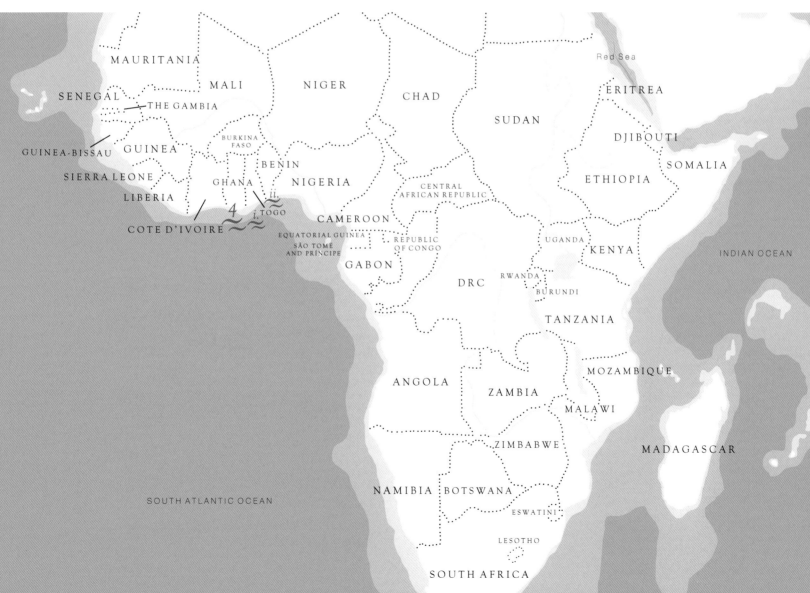

Indestructible Stoke on the Outskirts of Lagos

Tarkwa Bay,
Nigeria

Tarkwa Bay is a small sandy strip of man-made beach located just outside the entrance of Nigeria's busiest port. There, a break wall creates perfect wedges—where incoming waves are refracted and magnified as they fold over onto the shore. This accidental gift from the city's civil engineers has spawned a lively surf scene. At its center are John Micheletti, an Italian who was born and raised in Nigeria, and Godpower Pekipuma, a Tarkwa local through and through. Both learned to ride waves in the bay and have spent the last decade passing their passion on to kids from the village through free lessons, with another Nigerian, Rachel Ola, taking on a similarly leading role in recent years.

Under their guidance, the lineup has blossomed into a hotbed of raucous camaraderie, with dozens of young surfers trading off a limited quiver of donated broken and repaired boards, and a limitless supply of stoke. When waiting for a turn they line the breakwater, heckling and cheering as their buddies pull in just a stone's throw away. The fast, powerful, and often barreling waves have proved fertile ground for swift progression, fostering a deep pool of local talent, spurred on by friendly rivalries.

In 2019, Vans team riders Dylan Graves and Dane Gudauskas visited Tarkwa Bay, creating a joyous profile of the community for the web series Weird Waves, while photographer Oli Hillyer-Riley immortalized the trip in the book *No Wahala*. The response from the wider surfing world was one of equal jubilation, as viewers reveled in the

discovery of such a spirited grassroots scene in this little-known part of the surfing world.

In January 2020, just a few weeks after the episode was released, Tarkwa's peaceful vibe was shattered by a series of violent and unlawful evictions carried out by the Nigerian Navy. They arrived without warning, firing bullets into the air before bulldozing homes and businesses. Their stated aim was to halt the widespread theft of oil from the pipelines that pass nearby, yet thousands of innocent people were left destitute in their wake. Some locals believe the accusations were a front to mask the government's desire to clear the village to make way for luxury resorts.

After the evictions, the navy took control of the entire area. While most residents were forced to relocate, for the many local surfers who earn their

crust serving tourists on the beach, leaving was not an option. With their homes gone, they sought makeshift accommodations wherever they could. Some moved into tents, others simply picked a shady spot between the beach shacks.

Two years on and the community has returned to a state of delicate equilibrium. The navy is still there. But the locals have found ways to operate within the new system. Despite political uncertainties, Micheletti says the surf community is hopeful about the future, with many harboring aspirations to travel to Ghana or Senegal for competitions sometime soon. For now though, they're content to paddle out next to the break wall and simply take each wedge as it comes. ∼

No matter where you're from in the world, the morning surf check goes off much the same. Here, Californian Dane Gudauskas and Tarkwa local Emanuel compare notes while scouring the lineup for the best-looking peak (top, right). Dylan Graves hits the lip at Lighthouse Left, located on the other side of the breakwater from Tarkwa's famed right-hand wedge (opposite).

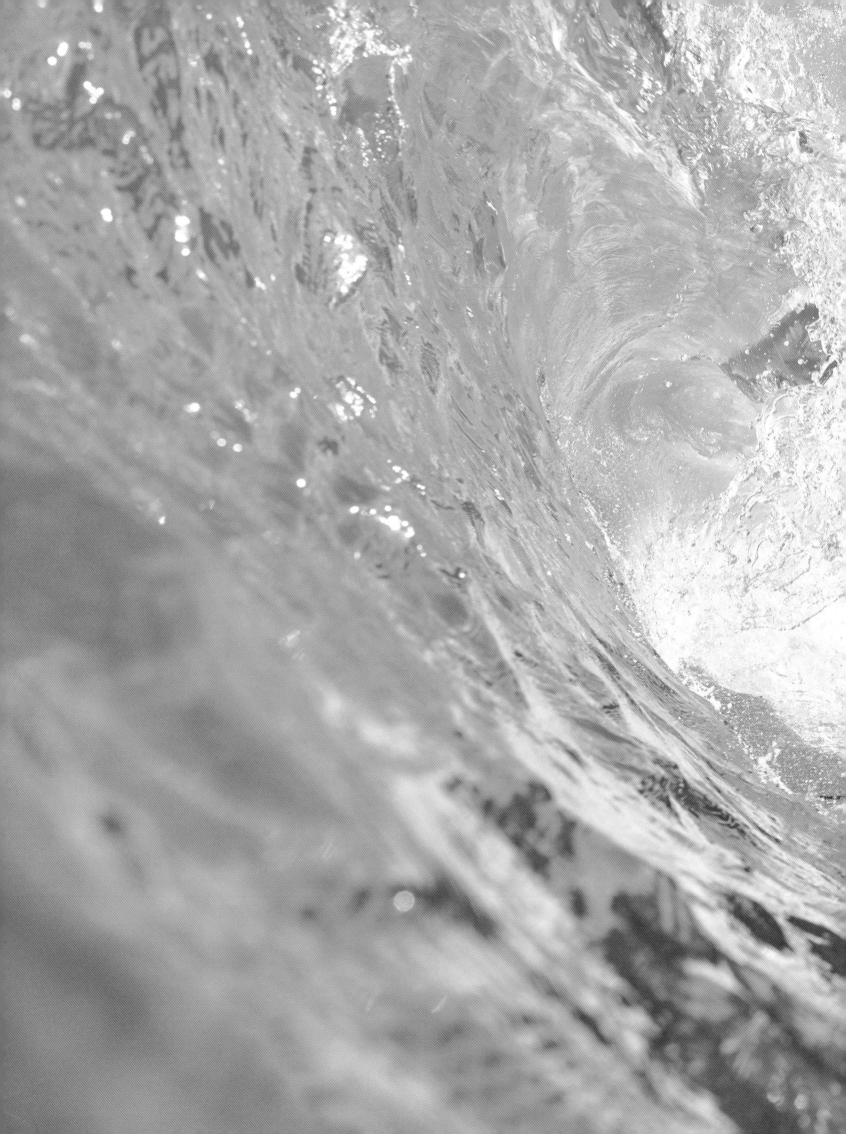

Local surfer Michael Gabriel, eyes trained down the line (previous spread). Taiye "Abraham" Kpossu (below and opposite) is one of the many groms Micheletti has supported and encouraged from a young age. During their visit, the Weird Waves crew were blown away by the speed at which he was able to replicate maneuvers he'd just been shown for the first time. "He's a natural talent," concluded Graves.

What You Need to Know

Level:
Beginner to expert.

Best time to visit:
May to September serves up regular waves in the waist- to head-high range.

What to bring:
With sea temperatures hovering around 80 °F (26.6 °C) all year round, you'll only ever need your favorite warm water surf attire.

What to do when it's flat:
Hop on a water taxi to Lagos where you'll find plenty to keep you occupied in one of the world's fastest-growing cities.

Local tip:
Tarkwa Bay now has two surf schools: GP, owned and operated by Godpower Pekipuma, and Black Girls Surf, run by Rachel Ola.

The plus to surf:
i. São Tomé Island, São Tomé and Príncipe; ii. Port-Gentil Area, Gabon

Treasure and Treachery in the Fortunate Isles

Canary Islands, Spain

Located just over 62 miles (100 kilometers) off the west coast of Africa, the Canary Islands are ideally placed to receive powerful swells from the North Atlantic, which lurch out of deep water and land with a punch on the archipelago's abundance of reefs and beaches.

The most famous spots are in the village of La Santa, on the northeast coast of the island of Lanzarote. The crowning glory, a shallow slab called El Quemao, delivers some of the best left-hand barrels in the whole of Europe, while Morro Negro throws up freight-train rights just a stone's throw away. On the island of Fuerteventura, a dirt road known as the North Track carves a course through the barren lunar landscape, linking many of the island's best spots, from El Cotillo on the west coast to Corralejo on the east. Just offshore, the island of Lobos produces long right-handers at the base of an extinct volcano. On the south coast of Tenerife, the bustling resort of Playa de las Américas plays host to numerous fun reef breaks, while over on Gran Canaria, the capital city of Las Palmas offers a variety of peaks along a sandy stretch called Las Canteras.

Dozens of other less well-known spots dot the islands, from the hard-to-reach slabs of Gran Canaria's north coast to the secluded reefs of La Palma, the best of which was recently destroyed by lava spewing from the Cumbre Vieja volcano.

Often compared to Hawaii thanks to its climate and topography, the Canaries' fledgling surf community was deeply inspired by the waterman spirit of their brothers in the Pacific. As a result, many of the island's earliest trailblazers in the 1970s were not only fearless big-wave specialists but also expert fishermen and seafarers too. Among the most legendary was Sergio "El Halcón" ("the Falcon") who returned from a stint sailing in the Pacific to pioneer El Quemao, while living in a cave just beyond the tideline. Their legacy remains, with the Canaries continuing to serve as a stomping ground for Europe's most dynamic watermen and women. ~

While each island is home to its own distinct coastal landscape, from plunging cliffs to rolling sandy plains, powerful waves over shallow lava rocks are a common feature throughout (above). Vilayta drops in at an undisclosed location (below) and Matias Hernandez lays back in Las Americas, Tenerife (opposite). The long rights of Los Lobos, captured from atop Montaña La Caldera (next spread).

What You Need to Know

Level:
Intermediate to expert.

Best time to visit:
For warm weather and the best chance of pumping waves, go from November to February.

What to bring:
A spare set of fins, in case of a dalliance with the shallow reefs.

What to do when it's flat:
Explore one of the numerous national parks, hike up a volcano, or take a sailing tour around the islands' secret beaches.

Fun fact:
The Canaries are composed of eight main islands, each formed by volcanic eruptions that began more than 20 million years ago.

The plus to surf:
i. Western Sahara; ii. Agadir Area, Morocco

Africa's Uncharted Isle

Madagascar

Madagascar is home to an extraordinary diversity of flora and fauna, much of which evolved in complete isolation after its separation from Africa 150 million years ago.

In more modern times, an Indigenous wave-riding culture has similarly flourished without outside influence, particularly among the Vezo people. Traditionally nomadic fisherfolk, they possess a mastery for navigating the treacherous reefs in their small dugout boats. Along the west coast, kids can be found riding the shore breaks on balsa wood and rough-hewn baobab. Far from being seen as an unwelcome distraction, surfing is positively encouraged among Madagascar's

Vezo youth, as a great way to hone the knowledge and skills needed for a life among the waves.

Ecstatic kids notwithstanding, Madagascar remains one of the Indian Ocean's most uncrowded surf destinations, thanks to its reputation for sharks, malaria, and difficult coastal access. There are some known outposts that attract a smattering of tourists and locals: in the southwest, Toliara is home to hard-breaking waves over live coral, and in the southeast, Taolagnaro (formerly known as Fort Dauphin), offers a mix of reefs and beaches that swirl up consistent swells from the Indian Ocean.

The country's remote northeast coast, however, remains largely uncharted. So, naturally, it was here that an intrepid crew of South Africans headed in 2015, with Alan van Gysen behind the lens. Because mountains covered with tangled vegetation abut much of the coast, the crew opted for a sea-bound expedition, setting sail in an audacious search for waves.

They returned with many and varied stories—from putting up tents on the edge of the forest in torrential rain to narrowly averting catastrophe when the boat got caught on a reef. But when, after a long fortnight, the crew finally headed for the comforts of home, they took with them a few cherished discoveries and a profound understanding of all that must be endured to truly explore the world's last untapped surf zones. ∽

After several days of exploring the region by boat, the team arrived in a V-shaped bay, home to a promising-looking pair of reefs on either side of a deep channel (previous spread, right). Their best discovery was a fun right-hander located a little further south. Here, Frank Solomon samples its hollow section (previous spread, left) while Slade Prestwich whacks the lip (opposite).

The northeastern coast of Madagascar is defined by extreme rainfall that sees the hilly landscape painted a lush shade of green all year round (above). An unpredictable coastal road links a series of small towns, where the abundant fruits of both the land and sea sustain populations largely cut off from the wider world (opposite).

What You Need to Know

Level:
Intermediate to expert.

Best time to visit:
For the east coast, November to March, for the west coast, April to November.

What to bring:
A wearable shark repellent and malaria tablets.

What to do when it's flat:
Visit the striking Avenue of the Baobabs, home to two dozen of the iconic African trees, some of which are several thousand years old.

Local tip:
If you're planning a trip to the reefs on the west coast, those in the know say you'll need at least two full weeks for a decent shot at getting a swell, even during peak season.

The plus to surf:
i. Inhambane Area, Mozambique; ii. Mauritius

Asia

1 *Siargao, Philippines*
2 *Mentawai Islands, Indonesia*
3 *Taitung, Taiwan*
4 *Kerala, India*
5 *Ramin, Iran*
6 *Oman*

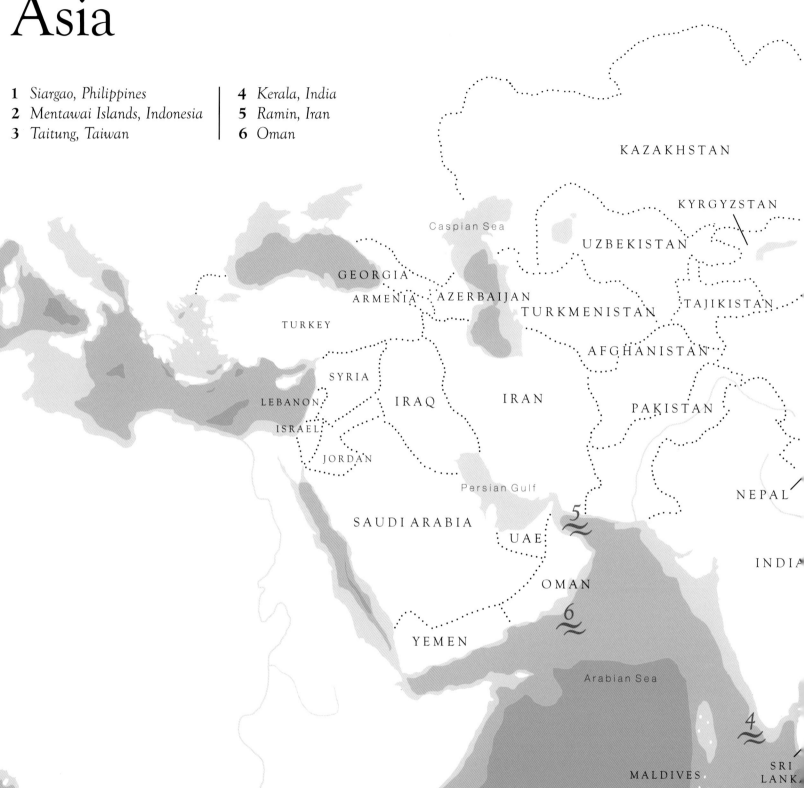

RUSSIA

KAZAKHSTAN

KYRGYZSTAN

Caspian Sea

UZBEKISTAN

GEORGIA

ARMENIA · AZERBAIJAN

TAJIKISTAN

TURKMENISTAN

TURKEY

AFGHANISTAN

SYRIA

LEBANON

IRAQ

IRAN

PAKISTAN

ISRAEL

JORDAN

NEPAL

Persian Gulf

SAUDI ARABIA

UAE

5

INDIA

OMAN

6

YEMEN

Arabian Sea

4

MALDIVES

SRI
LANKA

MONGOLIA

NORTH KOREA

JAPAN

SOUTH KOREA

CHINA

HUTAN

GLADESH

MYANMAR

LAOS

TAIWAN

3

Philippine Sea

Bay of
Bengal

THAILAND

South China Sea

VIETNAM

1

NORTH PACIFIC OCEAN

CAMBODIA

PHILIPPINES

BRUNEI

MALAYSIA

Celebes Sea

2

SINGAPORE

INDONESIA

PAPUA NEW GUINEA

Java Sea

Banda Sea

INDIAN OCEAN

Perpetual Flux in the Philippine Sea

Siargao,
Philippines

Of all the legends that underpin the discovery of the world's great surf breaks, few tales are as dramatic as that of Cloud Nine, a sublime right-hand reef break on Siargao Island in the Philippines.

According to lore, the wave's original pioneer was an American vagabond named Mike Boyum, a man famous for his global drug smuggling escapades throughout the 1970s and '80s. After a short prison stint in New Caledonia, in December 1988, Boyum followed a tip from two surfers he met in a bar, arriving under alias on Siargao's then deserted Tuason Point.

He spent the next few months living in a wooden hut on the beach, surfing the waves out front, meditating, and enduring long fasts, surviving solely on water and lemon juice delivered to him by the local villagers. After one perilously long spell, in June 1989, a group arrived to find him dead from starvation.

It wasn't until four years later that the barreling right in front of his hut was rediscovered by two American pros and photographer John Callahan, as they explored the coast by boat. Oblivious to the strange demise of their fellow countryman, they named the wave Cloud Nine after a local chocolate bar, a stroke that, given Boyum's cause of death, feels fiercely ironic in retrospect.

Fast-forward three decades and from these macabre and macho origins, a richly diverse and inclusive local surf scene has emerged. Beyond the dozens of rippers who frequent Cloud Nine on every swell, the island has also fostered a →

→ burgeoning crop of female longboarders, who fan out across its many mellower breaks.

At the forefront are the eminently talented sisters Ikit and Aping Agudo, and Josie Prendergast—a freesurfer and contemporary icon of women's longboarding. Born in Siargao but raised in Byron Bay, Prendergast has been returning to her birthplace at every opportunity in recent decades, encouraging more women into the waves and becoming a high-profile ambassador for Siargao's female surf crew.

Despite facing some of the same cultural and infrastructural struggles that confront every rapidly developing island hotspot, according to most, Siargao was a wonderful place to be throughout the late 2010s. Then, just as the island was gearing up to welcome tourists back after the pandemic hiatus, catastrophe struck.

In December 2021, Super Typhoon Odette tore through the Philippines, causing widespread devastation and leaving hundreds dead. On Siargao, surfers quickly mobilized to help with the relief efforts. A fundraising appeal led by Prendergast was met with an immediate outpouring of support from the global community, who donated over 80,000 AUD within just a few months.

It's clear it'll be a long road ahead for the many locals whose livelihoods were destroyed by the storm. But at the time of writing, some of the island's businesses are preparing to reopen and there are positive signs that—thanks to their unyielding resolve—the community is well on its way to restoring their island paradise. ∿

The local grom crew at Tuason Beach (top, left). Although famed for its perfect tubes, Cloud Nine produces great longboarding waves on smaller days.
Here, surf instructor Maricel Parajes takes full advantage (top, right).

The viewing tower at Cloud Nine was one of many structures completely destroyed by the typhoon. However, thanks to a community effort, it's well on its way to being rebuilt (above). As one of the island's most celebrated surf stars, Ikit Agudo was instrumental in raising funds and awareness around the plight of residents following the disaster (below).

What You Need to Know

Level:
Intermediate to expert.

Best time to visit:
Swells can arrive at any time, but most hit between July and December. Clean conditions are most likely in October and November, making those months prime time for a surf trip.

What to bring:
Avoid contributing to the problem of waste on the island by arriving armed with your own reusable water bottle and coffee cup.

What to do when it's flat:
Take a tour through the mangrove forest or go diving in the outer islands.

Local tip:
The General Luna fiesta takes place in September and is a great way to immerse yourself in the local culture and traditions.

The plus to surf:
i. Catanduanes; ii. Northern Mindanao

The Surfer's Reverie

Mentawai Islands,
Indonesia

Off the coast of West Sumatra, the Mentawai archipelago is modern surfing's most coveted playground,
home to dozens of peerless reef breaks backed by
pristine tropical scenery.

Much of the archipelago's potential was first
mapped by prolific surf adventurer Martin Daly,
who spent the 1980s and '90s crisscrossing the
Indian Ocean in a salvage boat, funding his travels
by diving on shipwrecks and recovering sunken
treasure along the way. Although the most high-
profile, he wasn't the only surfer on the islands.
Legend has it that in 1991 when Daly pulled up
to a wave on the southern tip of Sipora Island,
a man emerged from the jungle with a surfboard
and paddled out to greet him. It was Australian
Lance Knight, who'd arrived a few weeks earlier,
and had come across the spot while out exploring
with a local in a dugout canoe. The wave became
known as Lance's Right and to this day is
considered among the most perfect in Indonesia.

The Mentawai's surf history involves many
such intrepid characters who often attempted to
keep their discoveries well under wraps. But by the
mid-1990s, the word was out, and a battalion of
mostly foreign-owned charter boats were tooled up
and ready to whisk adequately affluent surfers out
to visit the islands. Land-based surf camps have
since emerged, but liveaboard boat trips remain the
ultimate experience, thanks to the flexibility and
total immersion they offer. For better and worse,
such tours have less impact on the environment,
population, and economy of the archipelago, as
surfers rarely touch land while on board.

While only a tiny percentage of surfers will
ever get to ride spots like Greenbush, Rifles, and
Macaronis, they have played a profound role in
establishing our collective definition of the perfect
wave and the perfect surf-trip routine. That is, to
pull up in the channel, leap overboard into warm
water, and return only once fully gorged on big
blue tubes, to share sunset beers and detailed
accounts of each ride long into the starry night. For
those seeking this enduring fantasy, there remains
no better place on earth than the Mentawai. ∽

While many visitors to the Mentawai remain aboard charter boats, Aussie Marc Llewellyn used his time working as resident photographer at Pitstop Hill resort to explore the country beyond the coast. Here, he photographs a makeshift bridge on Nyang Nyang Island (opposite), a surfer at a nearby wave named Bankvaults (above), and a tribesman named Aman LauLau on Siberut Island (below, right).

Each day, a fleet of small boats set out from the various land-based resorts around Nyang Nyang Island to find the best spot for the day's conditions (above). The Uma is a traditional Mentawai home, with a thatched roof and a veranda at each end (below). Visiting Californian Tom Morat ditching the fins at a playful left-hander known as Beng Bengs (opposite).

What You Need to Know

Level:
Intermediate to expert.

When to visit:
The main swell season runs from May to September. But the shoulder season, from October to March, still offers the chance for plenty of great surf in the head-high range with offshore winds and fewer crowds.

What to do when it's flat:
If you're on a boat trip, snorkeling, fishing, stand-up paddling, and heated card games are the most common forms of flat-day fun.

What to bring:
Pack mosquito repellent and a first aid kit, complete with antiseptic cream and plenty of aloe vera for inevitable reef cuts.

Local tip:
Looking to give back? Check out SurfAid and Waves For Water to find out how you can have a positive impact.

The plus to surf:
i. Bukit Peninsular, Bali; ii. West Java, Java

Taiwan's Green and Pleasant Coast

*Taitung,
Taiwan*

Sitting just off China's east coast, the island of
Taiwan features a striking contrast of high-rise cities,
mountainous national parks, and dense lowland
forests. Out beyond the shoreline, the sparse crowds,
tropical water temperatures, and rich variety of
breaks make it one of Asia's most underrated surf
destinations.

The waves were first ridden regularly by U.S.
soldiers stationed in the country after the Second
World War. One day in the early 1960s, a Taiwanese
boy named Mao Guh spotted a group out surfing
near the base where his father worked in the north.
One offered Guh a go on his board and from that
day on he was hooked. Martial law in the country
meant access to the ocean was strictly banned
for civilians but Guh continued to surf with the
soldiers throughout his teenage years. In 1969,
he opened the country's first surf shop.

Even after restrictions were lifted in the late
1980s, a culturally ingrained fear of the ocean
meant surfing was slow to take off. But in the last
decade, attitudes have finally begun to shift, thanks
in part to the concerted efforts of people like Baybay
Niu—one of the country's surf pioneers, who spent
years offering free surf lessons to local kids. Another
boon was the introduction of an international
surfing event, which has been running every year
since 2010 at Jinzun Harbor in the beautiful
Taitung region.

The town marks the capital of the east-coast
surf scene, with several more high-quality spots
located nearby. There's Cheng Gong, a barreling
left that needs a powerful swell to get going but
is considered one of the best spots in the country.
And Donghe Rivermouth, a consistent break that
shapes all available swell into long, fun walls and
occasional tube rides.

Traveling south from the town, many more
reefs and river mouths await, all serviced by a scenic
highway that snakes along the coast, offering the
potential to find your own pumping little corner
if the stars align. ~

"When we traveled to Taiwan, we didn't know what to expect," says photographer Matt Power, "turning up with zero knowledge of the area and waves. After some time exploring up the coast, we found this spot. We walked down through the palms and couldn't believe our eyes. A perfect little point break all to ourselves for the day. It's sessions like these that make all the effort worthwhile." (previous spread and above)

After requalifying for the World Tour in 2019, half Japanese, half Aussie surfer Connor O'Leary decided a typhoon-chasing trip to Taiwan was the perfect way to celebrate. He invited along photographer Matt Power to document proceedings and good buddy Shane Campbell for a bit of company round the campfire (opposite).

What You Need to Know

Level:
Beginner to expert.

Best time to visit:
The biggest typhoon swells arrive sporadically between July and September, while October to March sees a more consistent procession of groundswells. December to February is prime time for a visit.

What to bring:
Your warm-water surf gear! Since temperatures seldom drop below 73 °F (23 °C), you'll only need a spring wetsuit in the dead of winter.

What to do when it's flat:
Visit Dulan, an artistic and cultural hub located 12 miles (19 kilometers) north of Taitung City.

Local Tip:
Refuel after a long surf with a delicious steamed baozi bun from a local bakery.

The plus to surf:
i. Okinawa, Japan; ii. JeJu Do, South Korea

Surfing in the Spice Garden

*Kerala,
India*

Known as the Spice Garden of India, the coastal state of Kerala stretches verdantly along the country's southwestern edge. The landscape is defined by lush mountain ranges and a tangle of inland waterways that eventually give way to the Arabian Sea along 360 miles (579 kilometers) of sandy, palm-backed coast.

While the city of Kovalam is home to India's most long-established surf scene, a new Keralan heartland has recently taken shape just a few hours north. Centered on the town of Varkala, a string of breaks buzz with the enthusiasm of a first-generation surf community, while beachside retreats like Soul & Surf welcome visitors into the fray.

The shape of the shoreline fluctuates constantly, thanks to a tumultuous monsoon season, which blasts sediment southward from June until August. During this period, big swells close out many of the ruler-straight beaches, making it a dicey time for a surf trip. Most travelers prefer the season from September to May, when small swells from the Arabian Sea serve up consistent waist-to-shoulder-high waves that slowly replenish the sandbanks. The wind is generally light or offshore first thing, before the heat draws in the sea breeze around mid-morning.

At the region's premiere break, a left-hand point called Edava, this means the main surf window coincides with the return of the village's fishing fleet, who head straight in through the lineup. Elsewhere this might lead to conflict, but here there's an unspoken custom observed by both locals and visitors: surfers leave the water and help the fisherfolk haul their nets and boats up the beach. In uniting the foreshore's newest arrivals with those who've worked it for hundreds of years, this ritual embodies the synergy between tradition and modernity that defines so much of life in Kerala. ～

Local surf instructor Varghees Antony races a cascading lip at Edava (previous spread, right). Early mornings at the break are a hive of activity, with surfers, fisherfolk, and hungry sea birds all dancing to the tune of the Arabian Sea (opposite). Kerala's rolling green interior has been producing some of the world's most sought-after spices since 3000 BCE (below).

Just a few years after learning to surf as a teenager at Soul & Surf's Sunday club, Praveen Vs joined the team as an instructor. More recently he's developed into an accomplished longboarder, instantly recognizable for his relaxed and stylish approach in the Edava bowl (above).

What You Need to Know

Level:
Beginner to expert.

Best time to visit:
For consistent waist-to-shoulder-high waves accompanied by morning offshores, go between September and May.

What to bring:
Sometimes the power goes out during heavy downpours, so a good headlamp and flashlight are recommended.

What to do when it's flat:
Take a yoga class or get an Ayurvedic massage.

Fun fact:
Kovalam was the site of one of the world's first artificial surfing reefs. For a short time it was successful in creating good waves, but after a typhoon dislodged part of it from the seafloor it never broke properly again.

The plus to surf:
i. Lakshadweep Islands; ii. South-West Sri Lanka

The Pioneering Women of Iranian Surfing

Ramin,
Iran

Chabahar County occupies the easternmost stretch of Iran's coastline, reaching toward the border with Pakistan. Long believed to be a dangerous place, until recently entry required special permission and tourism in the region was almost nonexistent. In the last 10 years, it's become the unlikely home of Iran's first surfing outpost, in the small village of Ramin, where a sandy beach hosts consistent waves throughout the summer.

The area's potential was discovered by Irish surfer Easkey Britton, who became the first woman ever to ride the country's waves in 2010. Three years later she returned, this time inviting two Iranian sportswomen to accompany her to the coast: Shahla Yasini, a diver and lifeguard, and Mona Seraji, the country's first female snowboard instructor. As Britton taught them to pop up on the beach in Ramin, kids rushed down from the village to have a go—so she taught them too. When Britton left, Yasini and Seraji established a surf club and continued to hold regular sessions.

Although enthusiastic, the locals faced more challenges than beginners from elsewhere—in particular the women, who, according to Yasini, struggled to access practical surfwear that complied with the legal requirement for them to be completely covered.

After watching a documentary on Britton's 2013 excursion, Italian photographer Giulia Frigieri decided to make her own project. On her first visit in 2017, she struck up a friendship with Yasini, making two further trips in the years that followed. Each time, she found the surf scene in a new stage of development.

In 2013, Shahla Yasini (top, left) and Mona Seraji became Iran's first female surfers when Easkey Britton introduced them to the sport while over on a trip from her home in Ireland. When photographer Giulia Frigieri arrived four years later, a small surf scene had emerged in the town of Ramin (bottom, left) with regular workshops for locals and visitors from Tehran (top and bottom, right).

By 2019, Ramin was a popular spot, which brought with it clear improvements for the local people, but also the establishment of a government-controlled surf association. During Frigieri's final trip to the area, she was told she could no longer take pictures of men and women in the waves together.

While her photographs radiate the joy of a fledgling surf scene, it's impossible to disconnect them from the wider political context, particularly since each had to be reviewed and approved by state censors. Women's rights in Iran are severely limited, a fact that frequently prevents them from engaging in sports. Against such a backdrop, it might seem strange that the government has allowed, and even encouraged, surfing to take place at all.

Intriguingly, Yasini believes that the official support may stem from the same thing that caught the eye of the media outlets that ran images of her under headlines such as, "The Hijabi Surfers Making Waves in Iran."

"The idea of a documentary showing Iranian women surfing with hijab was attractive to the authorities," Yasini told journalist Haleh Anvari, in an essay published by *Aperture*. Why? Because it seemed to demonstrate that the legal requirement for women to be covered was not a limitation. As such, the photographs serve as a pertinent reminder of how surfing can be a medium for greater individual freedom—but also harnessed as a promotional tool by those looking to achieve altogether different aims. ⌁

Since Frigieri's first visit in 2017, the scene has continued to grow, with more Iranians entering the lineup thanks to regular coaching workshops hosted by the Davin Adventure Group (above).

What You Need to Know

Level:
Beginner to expert.

Best time to visit:
*June to August offers the best chance of scoring, while
November to April is usually totally flat.*

What to bring:
Bring boards, wax, fins, leashes, and all other surf supplies.

What to do when it's flat:
*Check out the amazing Martian Mountains or strange
Pink Lagoon.*

Local tip:
*There are reports of a top-class point break near the Maahi
fish cannery, just outside of Chabahar, but access from
the land is impossible, so you'll need to convince someone
to take you in a boat.*

The plus to surf:
i. West Pakistan; ii. East Oman

Chasing Mirages in the Empty Quarter

Oman

Slotted neatly on the eastern edge of the Arabian Peninsula, Oman's extensive coastline and unique blend of cultures has seen it become the epicenter of Middle Eastern surfing in recent years.

Although there are rare good days in the Gulf of Oman, the most popular surfing coast extends south from the village of Ras Al Hadd, facing out into the Arabian Sea. Here, a bevy of point breaks produce long, mellow waves consistently from April to September, when typhoons whip up swells from the south. Surfers from Dubai were these lineups' first regulars, with a small crew frequently making the nine-hour dash across the desert to greet summer swells throughout the early 2000s. More recently, a surf club was established by a group of Filipino expats and Omanis based in Muscat, who began organizing expeditions down the east coast, lending out equipment and encouraging kids into the surf, sowing the seeds for a resident community that has been growing steadily ever since.

To the south of the tiny, wave-rich Masirah Island, hundreds of miles of mostly deserted coastline zigzag all the way to the city of Salalah. This stretch marks the boundary between the Arabian Sea and one of the largest, most inhospitable deserts on earth; an undulating expanse known as the Empty Quarter. Along the coast, the country's otherwise pristine roads give way to nothing but sand dunes, navigable only by camel or 4 × 4. Tall cliffs fall away into turquoise waters, which remain crystal clear until the summer sandstorms swirl into the waves, creating a murky hue that conceals an array of marine wildlife, including turtles, stingrays, and several breeds of shark.

While much of the surfing potential of this region remains mysterious, a notable mission took place in June 2010 as the ferocious Cyclone Phet made landfall on the coast. For 10 days, a small convoy of international surfers, accompanied by photographer Sergio Villalba, searched for waves down desert tracks and camped out under the stars. They encountered no one but a few fisherfolk and local Bedouin, but in fleeting moments, found exactly what they were looking for just offshore.

Their greatest discovery was a fast barreling right-hander, tucked away in just one of several dozen similar inlets—a find that suggests, for those willing to endure blistering heat, fickle winds, and many nights at the mercy of the desert, Oman may still hold many great waves yet to be pioneered. ⌒

Brett Barley finds some shade between white hot rock and a shimmering horizon (opposite). Oman's desert plains demand a no-frills surf excursion, where everything required must fit into the back of your vehicle or in an improvised roof box (top, right). Sleeping and cooking arrangements are similarly spartan (bottom, right).

Wide bays, punctuated by rocky outcrops and sweeping sandy points make for a coastline rich in potential surf spots (above). Spaniard Pablo Gutierrez locks eyes with a section as he spring-loads off the bottom (below and opposite).

What You Need to Know

Level:
Beginner to expert.

Best time to visit:
To avoid the hottest, windiest months of the summer swell season, plan a trip for May or September.

What to bring:
Despite bath-water warm sea temperatures, sometimes you'll need a wetsuit because of the wind chill.

What to do when it's flat:
Spend a day with a Bedouin family and learn about their rich cultural history.

Local tip:
Locally grown coffee and dates are always served to guests upon arrival—a cornerstone of Oman's culture of hospitality.

The plus to surf:
i. North Yemen; ii. West Pakistan

Chasing the Ghosts: of a Surfing Dream

Ever since people first rode waves they've followed compulsions and dreams to find better ones. For surfers, the ideal of the perfect wave burns in their mind. It's this endless search that makes surfing unique; a dream that built a culture. But does the perfect wave exist? And if so, do we really want to find it?

BY JAMIE P. CURRIE

Looking For Something to Find

You might say that surfing's never really been about riding waves. It's about searching. The search for the perfect wave is a symbol of our desire to keep looking for something to find. Just as Vikings sailed toward uncertain horizons fearing they might drop off the ends of the earth, so surfers have been compelled to reach into the unknown, searching for a perfection that may or may not exist.

The perfect wave is highly subjective. One person's Uluwatu is another's Skeleton Bay is another's Nazaré is another's Malibu. Each to their own. And when we finally created an artificial wave that looked like sheer perfection, it turned out it wasn't what we wanted at all. As in life, the journey is more important than the destination.

Really, there is no perfect wave. There's no end point to reach. What we are searching for are moments. All surfers have them, enshrined in their memories. Moments of such eidetic ecstasy that everything else falls away like shattered glass. This is all we can hope to find.

Turn On, Tune In, Drop Out

The earliest surfers likely took to the water out of curiosity and necessity. The first account of surfing is from the 1640s, and was written about the culture of wave riding in what is today known as Ghana. Around the world, surfers—from ancient Polynesian kings, to 10th-century Chinese river riders—may not have traveled far and wide for waves like we do today, but their journeys headed into something no less unknown. As for what they discovered, well, it was more like breaking ground toward a mysterious treasure we're still unearthing today.

155

It was the early 1960s when the flame of surf travel was blown to a blaze. The swashbuckling stories of Australian Peter Troy and the mainstream love affair with Bruce Brown's *The Endless Summer* were the symbols of this newfound ideal, but really the desire to expand hearts and minds in far-off lands was a mark of cultural and societal change that defined the '60s. Surfing was the perfect vehicle to turn on, tune in, and drop out.

In 1963, Peter Troy set off on a surf trip that would last four years. At a time when globetrotting travel was uncommon and fraught with difficulty, Troy's exploits are legendary. He journeyed through South America, the Middle East, Europe, and Africa using various means and methods, and mostly carrying a surfboard, an oddity he likened to "traveling the world carrying a grand piano." His strangeness in strange lands attracted luck and kindness. In a profile for *Surfing* magazine in 1987, Troy said he had visited 130 countries—38 in Africa alone. He remains a pioneering figure of surf travel lore. What he experienced on his travels was undoubtedly more than just a few good waves.

If Troy's stories are relatively niche within the world of surfing, in 1966, the documentary *The Endless Summer* was to change that, rocketing the dream of the perfect wave into mainstream consciousness. The stars of the film, Robert August and Mike Hynson, traveled the globe over a four-month period, their search for the perfect wave documented and narrated by filmmaker Bruce Brown. The climax of the film, when they stumble over dunes to discover what was considered to be the perfect wave of that era—a clean, 4-foot (1.2-meter) point break at Cape St. Francis, South Africa—is still the most iconic moment in surf film history. "On Mike's first ride," Brown says as proud narrator and instigator of a million dreams, "he knew he'd finally found that perfect wave."

Stumbling upon perfection was likely the high point of Mike Hynson's life. In the years following, he suffered from drug and alcohol problems, leading to time in jail and a period of homelessness. All of which questions whether finding the dream wave really is something we want at all; perhaps a dream's power relies on it remaining just out of reach.

How the Search Was Sold

The concept of the perfect wave took root in the surf world and never left. The entirety of surf media was built on it. Surfing magazines sold travel tales in every issue. Surf film narratives were almost exclusively centered around search and discovery. Brands were established with an apparent commitment to core surf values. Surf camp and boat trip industries emerged across the world as people continued to perpetuate what many felt to be a dying dream.

During the '70s and '80s surf-travel boom, the most intrepid adventurers were split into two clear factions: those who understood that what they'd found could make them money, and those who had the foresight to know it was too special to last.

The former saw the Indonesian archipelago transformed from a deserted surf paradise to a hub of global surf tourism almost overnight. Bali's proximity to Australia ensured it was the first to be mined. The mechanical and seemingly endless left-handers of Uluwatu became the new vision of the perfect wave, brought to the world in the 1972 film *Morning of the Earth*. More importantly, whispers of the region's potential for undiscovered surf ignited the imagination of surfers who descended on the islands like wasps on an open jam jar. Indonesian discoveries lasted decades, and even today there are occasional flickers. Padang Padang, G-Land, the Mentawais, Desert Point, Lakey Peak—all have been established as holding some of the world's best waves.

The great irony is that the search for waves and freedom has ruined many secret spots. The pioneers who just wanted to share what they'd found, in boastfulness or kindness, and the entrepreneurs who realized they could turn a buck from surfing, all put a bullet in the thing they loved.

There is a faction of committed surfers—perhaps even the majority—who still believe in the old dream and abhor the idea of surfing as something to be bought or sold. To them it is a simple expression of freedom, and perhaps a symbol of opaque purpose. Don't question or examine it, just do it because it feels good. The journey of surfing is personal, not for profit. And you keep searching because your perfect wave is still to be discovered. Dreams of adventure and travel lie at the heart of surf culture. It might be hopping from jungled island to deserted reef in the South Pacific, or whacking your way through old-growth forest in the Pacific Northwest. Or maybe, it's just camping out in your car above a hidden cove. Whatever your context, you're on the search. Thousands of surfers around the world are right there with you, chasing the ghosts of a surfing dream.

But this clash of ideals—the pursuit of profit versus joy—has created an unresolved issue. Spots have become increasingly crowded and surf culture suffers from a Jekyll and Hyde problem, a balancing act somewhere between bliss and fury. Today, there is a deep-rooted secrecy in surfing, which is somewhat ironic given geolocation and the capacity of →

Few real secrets remain, but ask surfers about their favorite spots and you might be met with a look like you've spat in their lunch. "Loose lips sink ships," as one photographer noted when we requested the locations of his submissions for this book.

Surfing is unique among action sports in that you spend far more time searching, preparing, and paddling than you do actually riding waves. The key to a happy surfing life is in learning to relish these in-between moments just as much.

→ the internet. Few real secrets remain, but ask surfers about their favorite spots, and you might be met with a look like you've spat in their lunch. "Loose lips sink ships," as one photographer noted when we requested the locations of his submissions for this book.

The Kingdom's All Inside

If there's a misconception about surfing, it's that the act of riding a wave is in some way useful, enlightening, even. Really it's about the most frivolous thing you can do. Sure, there are health benefits to being in the ocean. And there's no doubt something to be gained from a communion with the natural world and the love of nature it brings. But for many surfers, the real value has nothing to do with any of this. Over the course of a life, the time you'll spend actually riding waves borders on negligible.

The definition of perfection is surely something that remains just out of reach, and nowhere is that more apparent than in surfing. There are endless variables that might make a "perfect" wave, both physical and metaphysical. The true beauty of waves lie not in their perfection but their imperfection. That's what keeps us going. Because you know that whether you're seven or seventy, the greatest wave could still be ahead. And you'll always want more. The true joy of surfing is not the discovery of perfect waves, or even the search for them, but just the hope they might exist. So here's to the perfect wave—let's hope you never find it. ⁓

4
≈

Gulf of Alaska

ALEUTIAN ISLANDS

North America

1 *Mavericks, United States* | **3** *Tofino, Canada*
2 *Malibu, United States* | **4** *Alaska, United States*

NORTH PACIFIC OCEAN

CANADA

UNITED STATES

3
≈

1
≈

2
≈

MEXICO

California's Cold Coliseum

Mavericks,
United States

Mavericks is mainland America's most notorious big-wave spot—a terrifying blemish on California's "Surf City" veneer.

Mavericks is located half a mile (8 kilometers) off Pillar Point, where great whites patrol the murky lineup and freezing peaks fold over into an impact zone fringed by a field of jagged rocks. Some call it "the boneyard," others "the cheese grater," but all are aware that if you surf this wave, at some point you'll end up being driven in there by the full force of the North Pacific.

Those ominous shapes in the whitewash go some way to explaining why, despite its proximity to San Francisco, Mavericks remained mostly unridden for much of the 20th century. In fact, after it was first tackled in 1975, the wave was surfed by just one man for 15 years. His name is Jeff Clark, and the tales of his pioneering exploits are the stuff of surfing legend.

Growing up in Half Moon Bay, Clark attended the local high school, perched high on a hillside overlooking the point. Each winter, he'd watch giant empty waves breaking out toward the horizon, and as his surfing ability grew, his sights became set on riding them. One September day, aged just 17, he told his friend Brian he was paddling out. Brian declined to join him, as did all his other surf buddies. And so, for the decade that followed, Clark continued surfing Mavericks completely alone.

It wasn't until the early 1990s that he finally convinced a group of surfers from nearby Santa Cruz to come over for a look. Their accounts of the Hawaiian-sized waves that were breaking down the road were enough to inspire a few more visitors. Before Clark knew it, Mavericks was on the cover of *Surfer* magazine.

It was only then, as the collective race to push the limits of surfing began, that the true extent of the dangers of this big-wave spot became apparent. A few days before Christmas in 1994, a group of locals and Hawaiians converged for a swell. Among them was Mark Foo, known for his standout performances at Waimea. It was a clear morning, the lineup sparkling in the winter sun. After several successful rides, Foo spun and went on a 15-footer (4.5 meter), but fell on the takeoff and was quickly enveloped. His broken board surfaced in the whitewash and a few hours later his lifeless body was found floating in the lagoon. "It's not tragic to die doing something you love," he'd famously told an interviewer years earlier—but it was a dark day for the surf community and a chilling reminder of exactly what's at stake for every rider who decides to take on Mavericks.

In the decades after, the spot's notoriety continued to rise, with each wipeout and momentous ride building its reputation as the place where all big-wave surfers must go to prove themselves. From the new millennium onwards, each winter saw scores of new faces arrive on the peak. But in 2021, it was 51-year-old local devotee Pete Mel who snagged what is widely regarded as the best wave ever ridden at the break: a heart-stopping drop to giant tube that proved, when it comes to Mavericks, several decades of experience is far more potent than bright-eyed bravado and a young set of knees. ~

The view from Half Moon Bay across the harbor to Pillar Point, with a giant Mavericks A-frame breaking just beyond (previous spread). The regular pack features a real mix of surfers, from world-famous icons like Peter Mel (opposite), to underground local heroes like Matt Becker (top, right). A perspective revealing just some of the nasty rocks that wait to greet surfers on the inside (bottom, right).

Looking shoreward, air force satellites and the majestic mountains of the Rancho Corral de Tierra dominate the view from the lineup (above). Considered trickier and more dangerous than the famous right-hander, Mavericks' left has often been overlooked. However, in recent years, a small crew has sought to tame its hollow interior. Among the most successful is Will Skudin (below).

What You Need to Know

Level:
Big-wave experts only.

Best time to visit:
The biggest, most powerful swells arrive throughout the winter months, from November to March.

What to bring:
Most tackle Mavericks on big-wave guns, ranging in length from 9 to 11 feet (2.7 to 3.3 meters).

What to do when it's flat:
When Mavericks isn't breaking, there may still be fun surf at nearby Ocean Beach. If that's flat too, head for the bright lights of San Francisco.

Fun fact:
Mavericks was named in honor of a dog who paddled out after its owners during their attempt to ride waves on the inside at Pillar Point in the late 1960s.

The plus to surf:
i. Santa Cruz; ii. Santa Barbara

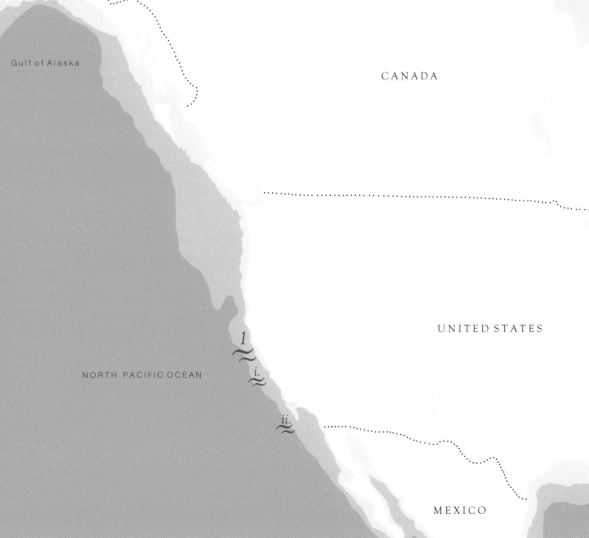

Gulf of Alaska

CANADA

NORTH PACIFIC OCEAN

UNITED STATES

MEXICO

Increments of Fear

in the Land of the Giants

The quest to ride the largest waves on the planet is one that few people can really understand, yet it never fails to draw our curiosity. Giant, ferocious waves are dotted around the globe, each with their own unique character and dangers. When fed by epic storm systems, they come to life—and when they do, a unique breed of surfer is poised to hunt them.

BY JAMIE P. CURRIE

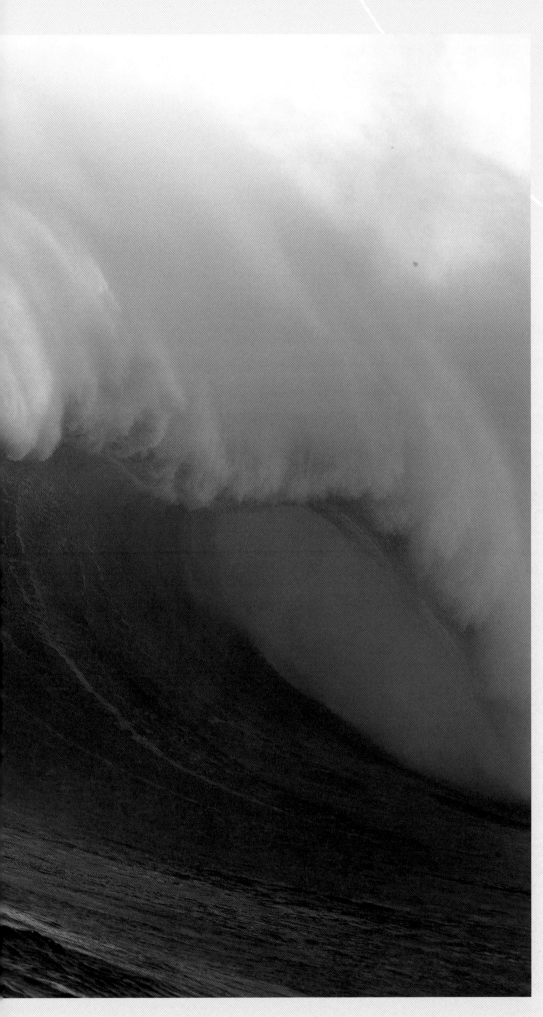

Albee Layer's approach at Jaws sums up the death or glory mindset of the modern big wave surfer. Over the last five years, he's accrued historic rides and near-fatal wipeouts in almost equal measure.

An Elemental Draw

If there's one element of surfing that never fails to captivate people, it's the pursuit of giant waves. Most of us will never know what it's like to harness the force of hundreds of tons of water. Or how it feels to confront your own mortality when driven beneath the water, tossed violently in the blackness with no sense of where the surface is, and feel as though your limbs might be torn from their sockets, and your lungs might explode in your chest.

Big-wave surfing is fearful in an innate way. Truly big surf has a primordial power, like a lion's roar; a deep, thundering growl that comes from somewhere unspeakable. It's the kind of sound you don't need to learn to fear. Giant waves detonating on reefs are not just heard by surfers, they are felt in the very core of their being. There's a misconception that big-wave surfers are driven by recklessness or bravery. Rather, it's fear that holds them in its grasp. Just like mountaineers and polar explorers before them, forging into the unknown and forever on the cusp of glory or death, so too these surfers keep paddling back out, senses alive in an elemental way few can understand.

Measuring Up

There is widespread conjecture among surf communities as to how waves should be measured and sizes defined. What surfers in one place might call 10 feet (3 meters), others might call 20 feet (6 meters). For the sake of argument, we might use the measurements of the largest waves ever surfed, as defined by the Guinness World Records, though not all surfers agree with them.

The record for the largest wave ever surfed is held by Germany's Sebastian Steudtner, for an 86-foot (26.2-meter) monster caught at Nazaré, Portugal, in October 2020. The women's record is held by Brazil's Maya Gabeira for a 73.5-foot (22.4-meter) wave ridden in February 2020 at the →

173

→ same location. This is closely followed by France's Justine Dupont, who caught a wave of 70.5 feet (21.5 meters) on the same day. The latter two waves are not only the largest waves ever caught by women, but also the fifth and sixth largest waves ever ridden.

Regardless of debates over size, when dealing with the most fearsome waves on earth a few feet either way hardly matters. Anyone who's been surprised by the power of waves less than head-high can tell you that.

Where Giants Fall

It's hard to pinpoint the exact origins of big-wave surfing. Its genesis exists largely as myth, carried only by oral traditions. The first time people were bold enough to paddle out into monstrous surf there were no cameras to freeze the moment, no journalists to relay the tales. There were only those who happened to be there, wide-eyed and fearful that the figures dwarfed by walls of water might never walk on land again.

What we do know is that it came to widespread attention at Waimea Bay on the North Shore of Oahu, Hawaii, thanks mostly to the fact that it was captured on film. In 1957, filmmaker Bud Browne shot footage of Californian Greg Noll and a small group of friends taking on the waves of Waimea Bay. This became a proving ground and remained this way until the early 1990s. Even though Waimea has long been eclipsed by spots where waves are bigger, better quality, and more consistent, it remains an icon of big-wave lore.

A Global Quest

Today the world's premier big-wave spots are spread far and wide, each with distinctive character and inherent dangers. Hawaiian legend Buzzy Trent's famous quip holds true: "Waves aren't measured in feet, but in increments of fear." Big-wave hunters have emerged in all corners of the globe, pushing these increments.

On the island of Maui, Hawaii, is Pe'ahi, more commonly referred to as "Jaws," where waves reach sizes of over 60 feet (18.3 meters) or more. It was here that tow-surfing was born, invented in the 1990s by a pioneering group of local surfers, including Laird Hamilton, Darrick Doerner, and Dave Kalama, who used jet skis to whip them into waves. Since then, Jaws has drawn widespread attention

for gold-standard enormous waves, perfectly formed and deadly in their beauty.

In California, a wave named Mavericks in Half Moon Bay is the scene of stories forever etched into big-wave history. A local surfer named Jeff Clark was the first to catch a wave at Mavericks when he was just 17. He paddled out alone with a homemade board, and it took 15 years for anyone to be brave enough to join him. Understanding Clark's boldness requires some context. Mavericks is not inviting. It is cold, dark, and faces a shoreline of jagged rocks. The wave, which reaches heights of up to 50 feet (15.2 meters), breaks violently onto a rock shelf, below which lie underwater caverns and fingers of reef that grab hold of leashes and limbs, trapping surfers who don't make the precipitous drop. Not only that, but the lineup is patrolled by great white sharks the size of small submarines.

Despite this, many have been drawn to it, including teenager Jay Moriarity, whose story was immortalized in the film *Chasing Mavericks*. Moriarity is also the subject of one of the most iconic surf pictures ever taken. In it, he is suspended in front of a pitching Mavericks lip, a full 30 feet (9.1 meters) in the air. His board is pointed directly to the sky, with only his outstretched arms visible, the resulting image conjuring the shape of a cross. He was just 16 years old when the picture was taken.

The next giant wave to capture the world's attention was found in Tahiti. Here, Teahupoo—a freak among freakish waves—redefined ideas of what big-wave surfing looked like. Just a third of a mile (5 kilometers) offshore, the ocean floor drops to 1,000 feet (305 meters), falling to 5,000 feet (1,524 meters) deep three miles out. The full force of distant Pacific Ocean swells collide with a shallow reef, sucking up water to create a wave with a trough below sea level and a lip so thick it's unlike anything else in the world.

At the turn of the century, Hawaiian surfer Laird Hamilton was towed into a wave that has become known as the Millennium Wave. It was a wave so alien, so unlike anything that had come before, that surf magazines scrambled to prove it was real before it eventually graced every cover. In photographs, Hamilton looks like he's encased in a giant cavern of glass. The lip is almost as thick as the wave face is tall, yet there is no hint of whitewater until it detonates on the reef. The images are arresting to this day.

Then, in the mid-2000s, a wave that had terrified fisherfolk for generations was unearthed by the international big-wave community in the small town of Nazaré, Portugal. Two factors have made Nazaré the center of the big-wave universe in recent years. The first is the geographical anomaly that creates the largest rideable waves on earth: a deep underwater canyon funneling the full power of wild Atlantic swells to the shore. The second is that people experience the spectacle of these waves in such close proximity that they might feel the spray on their faces. On days when men face monsters a stone's throw away, large crowds gather by the lighthouse on the cliff, creating a gladiatorial amphitheater. If any wave looks like it came straight from a comic book sketch, it's this one.

Evolution of a Perilous Art

Big-wave surfing has evolved into sub-genres based on equipment and waves. The major split is an aesthetic one: do you use a jet ski or do you prefer the purity of catching waves with your own paddle-in power?

Giant waves move faster than it is possible to paddle, so there is a natural limit to the size of wave rideable without assistance. Paddling speed and efficiency increases in proportion to the length and volume of the surfboard, so paddle-in surfing requires thick boards of 10 feet (3 meters) or more in length. Although these boards paddle well, their maneuverability is severely compromised when riding waves.

The introduction of the jet ski expanded the boundaries of what was possible with big waves. Tow-in surfboards are shorter than traditional equipment and include footstraps to give surfers more control and to facilitate tighter turns. This has enabled progressive big-wave surfers, such as Kai Lenny and Albee Layer, to perform aerial maneuvers and barrel rides on gigantic waves that would be impossible with paddle-in equipment.

Although tow-in surfing remains the only method of riding the largest waves on earth, it has led to a backlash from some purists who believe that paddle-in surfing is more in line with surfing's core values. There are key advocates on both sides of the debate, but many utilize the best of both worlds—paddle to a certain size, tow when it gets too big.

Regardless of personal tastes, the jet ski remains the most significant factor in the evolution and →

Hawaiian legend Buzzy Trent's famous
quip holds true: "Waves aren't measured
in feet, but in increments of fear."

→ safety of big-wave surfing. The dangers of big-wave surfing are many, but the number of deaths in the sport is perhaps fewer than expected. The addition of jet skis has been a major factor, as has the recent introduction of inflatable vests equipped with canisters of CO_2 that bring surfers back to the surface rapidly after a wipeout. The majority of big-wave surfers are extremely well prepared and approach their passion with a safety-conscious mindset. This kind of surfing is all about preparation and calculated risk.

Professional big-wave surfers are on red alert for generational storm systems, going as far as to race one epic swell from continent to continent, catching the same waves in different parts of the world. They train relentlessly, building muscle, lung capacity, and mental resilience, and are primed to drop everything if "that day" ever comes.

Finding the Limits

Big-wave surfing remains a primal chase to test human potential and cement yourself in legend. Despite mainstream interest, most big-wave surfers do it for the love, and in that context, it remains a relatively pure facet of surf culture. It's easy to see why it becomes addictive. The swells surfers are chasing could be a once-in-a-lifetime opportunity. Maybe even once in many lifetimes. One wave might assure your place in history. We still don't know what the biggest waves surfed are. Has anyone surfed a 100-foot (30-meter) wave? Some people might say yes, others absolutely no. It's not as straightforward as conquering mountains, because these mountains come and go and continue to grow.

While surfing big waves is often considered a testosterone-fueled pastime, times are changing. Led by surfers like Keala Kennelly, Paige Alms, Justine Dupont, and Maya Gabeira, women are tackling monster waves the world over. Though women may have taken longer to become a prominent feature of lineups, now that they are, they're certainly making their mark.

Today, the largest waves on the planet are still out there, waiting for the right variables to align. This makes chasing big waves a frustrating and somewhat idealistic endeavor. But if there's one thing we can be certain of, it's that surfers from all over the globe will continue to hunt them. ⌒

The First Perfect Wave

Malibu,
United States

The single most important spot in American surfing history throughout the '50s and '60s, Malibu was the center of the surfing universe. The spooling point break was as close to a perfect wave as anyone could imagine, birthing not just Southern Californian beach culture but the surfing explosion in mainland America as a whole. Malibu dictated both surfboard evolution and style. It's a wave that demands an economy of movement, down the line trim, and endless glide.

Many legends have come and gone at Malibu, but the stories of two characters in particular symbolize its rise and fall: Miki Dora and Kathy "Gidget" Kohner. There could scarcely be greater contrast between them, but both shared a love of Malibu that defined not just their lives but millions of others in their wake.

Kohner was a diminutive teenager with a joyful love of surfing. Her adventures at Malibu were part-fictionalized by her writer father, who wrote a best-selling novel about them, followed by successful movie and TV adaptations. This led to an American obsession with surfing that saw thousands of new surfers flock to the lineups, especially at Malibu.

Dora, on the other hand, was tall and dark—in looks and often mood—and for a time was the undisputed king of Malibu. He was famous for his smooth style on water and his hustler's lifestyle away from it. Indeed, he left behind a complicated legacy. As surfing boomed, he pronounced it dead, especially at Malibu. He fled the United States, hustling his way round the world, pursued by the FBI for fraud. Today, many regard him as a totem of the anti-establishment surfing lifestyle.

Malibu was once a dreamland where surfing was practiced with poise, grace, and joy. Today it has been upstaged in the annals of perfect waves, not least due to the crowd factor. It still represents an ideal, but one that is forever lost. Many surfers would still kill for a few perfect Malibu waves to themselves. As pioneering board designer Dale Velzy, says in Matt Warshaw's *The History of Surfing*: "Everybody looked good surfing there. It was always a very kind wave." Good luck getting one. ～

An original member of the Z-Boys surf and skate team, these days Allen Sarlo sits alongside Miki Dora and Kathy "Gidget" Kohner in Malibu's hall of fame (opposite).

What You Need to Know

Level:
Beginner to expert.

Best time to visit:
Any time there won't be a crowd.
Maybe during a pandemic?

What to bring:
An old-school longboard and
a beavertail wetsuit.

What to do when it's flat:
You're in Southern California; you should
find enough beautiful, famous, or crazy
people to entertain yourself people-watching
for a day or two.

Local tip:
Valley kooks go home!

The plus to surf:
i. South Los Angeles; ii. Orange County

Gulf of Alaska

CANADA

NORTH PACIFIC OCEAN

UNITED STATES

MEXICO

Movers and Shakers on Vancouver Island

Tofino,
Canada

Tofino sits at the tip of a thumb-shaped peninsula on Vancouver Island's mottled west coast. Surrounded by mountains, sea, and majestic old-growth cedar and fir, here, the built world is dwarfed by nature's grand architecture. Settlers arrived throughout the 1960s and '70s to work in the forest, dodge the Vietnam draft, and live closer to the land. Some holed up in shacks behind otherwise deserted beaches, and the few surfers among them set out to explore the coast's bounty of waves.

Several decades on and the seeds they planted have grown into an unlikely, but thriving, surf town. Equally instrumental in driving its development was the vision of two maverick event organizers.

The first was Dom Domic, who followed whispers of surfable waves to the sands of Long Beach in 1986. Back then, Tofino was still a hardcore fishing and logging hub, with virtually no tourism and a small, reclusive surf community. But after two years of getting acquainted with the place, Domic decided it was the perfect spot for a surf competition. Word spread quickly, and by its second year, hundreds of spectators descended on the coast for a weekend of revelry. After that, the landowner put a stop to proceedings. But those two years had been enough to open more than a few eyes to the region's surf potential.

By the time Domic returned to host his Surf Jam again a decade later (this time with the blessing of the park's authority), the local surf scene had blossomed. Now with big-brand backing, the annual event offered prize money and sponsorship opportunities, opening the door for the top locals to turn pro. The Bruhwiler siblings—Raph, Sepp, and Catherine—were never far from the podium, while a young up-and-comer named Pete Devries—son of an original '60s surf-shack owner—was often hot on their heels.

In 2009, when these grassroots affairs made way for an international event, the Cold Water Classic, Devries shocked the surfing world by storming past top competitors from Hawaii and Australia to victory. Of course, Domic was there, microphone in hand, bellowing with pride and adulation alongside a huge local crowd. From that day forth, Tofino was firmly on the surfing map.

The following year, an all-new event arrived to shake up the scene once again. Organized by Krissy Montgomery, Queen of the Peak (QOTP) set out to celebrate the town's exuberant crew of female surfers. Having spent years running the Surf Sister Surf School, it was a natural extension of Montgomery's desire to encourage more women into the lineup and get those already there the recognition they deserved.

Twelve years on and with the event still going strong, it's safe to say she's succeeded. Tofino is now home to hundreds of dedicated female shredders, including internationally renowned talent like the Olin sisters and Hanna Scott, who credits QOTP with driving the boom. "Before, there were no contests that made the women feel welcomed or taken seriously," she says. "It's been a pretty amazing evolution to watch." ~

Young ripper Sanoa Olin cracks one off the lip (top, left). At one of the region's best breaks, right-handers run off along a cobblestone point, as mountains and tufts of old-growth forest rise up all around (top, right). Although you'd never find it on the "care tips" label, hanging a wetsuit in front of a beach bonfire after a morning surf makes slipping into it for round two far more appealing (bottom, left).

Regional standout Pete Devries throws an arc of backlit spray at his local point break (above). Despite the freezing water temps and head-to-toe neoprene coverage, Hanna Scott finds plenty to smile about (below). Tofino experiences tidal ranges of up to 13 feet (4 meters), drastically altering the size and shape of the beaches over the course of the day (opposite).

What You Need to Know

Level:
Beginner to expert.

Best time to visit:
If you're after fun-sized waves and more settled weather, go from June to August, while for big swells and wild conditions, a winter trip's the one.

What to bring:
Carry bear spray with you in case of an encounter on a quiet beach or forest trail.

What to do when it's flat:
Tofino is world-famous for its whale-watching tours, with orcas and humpbacks regularly sighted in the Clayoquot Sound.

Local tip:
If the swell is small, head to Cox Bay. As the town's most exposed beach, it'll almost always have a little wave.

The plus to surf:
i. Northern Oregon, USA; ii. Humboldt County, USA

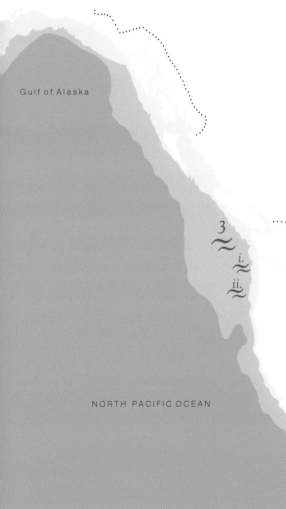

Gulf of Alaska

CANADA

NORTH PACIFIC OCEAN

UNITED STATES

MEXICO

North America's Fickle Frontier

Alaska,
United States

Located on the northwest extremity of North America, Alaska represents one of surfing's final frontiers. Over the past few decades, small groups of intrepid surfers have been journeying there to search for waves along its expansive and frigid coastline. Chief among them is Josh Mulcoy, originally from Santa Cruz, California, who became captivated by the region during his first visit in the early 1990s and has returned every year since. His favorite spot—an isolated fishing town he prefers not to name—features a fickle left-hand point break that peels down a sandbar, backed by the jagged snowy peaks of one of the world's tallest coastal mountain ranges. Inspired by contact with visitors like Mulcoy, the town now boasts a small local scene, complete with its own surf club and shop. Recently, some of the more experienced members of the community began hosting surf meetups as a way to introduce local kids to the joys of wave riding.

In 2019, Mulcoy invited some friends to join him on his annual trip to the region, including Oregon-based photographer Mark McInnis. While driving across a snow-covered beach one morning, the group's vehicle broke down, leaving them stranded on a section of coast they'd usually fly straight past. As they set about fixing the four-wheel drive, they spotted well-shaped waves, created by a freshly formed sandbar, breaking up ahead. A few days later, as a larger swell collided with the coast, they returned to find perfect surf breaking in the spot. "All I remember is hoots, screams, and boards getting ripped out of trucks," recalls McInnis of the moment they pulled up. "It was one of those moments where you think to yourself: 'I cannot believe I'm seeing this!'"

McInnis's images from the trip capture the sense of glorious serendipity that underpins every great surfing discovery, framed by the beautiful surroundings that, for Mulcoy at least, make every trip to the region worthwhile, regardless of the waves he finds. ⁓

Whether taking in the beauty of a deserted beach (above), gouging into a glassy runner (below), or collecting a dusting of snow on his wetsuit hood (opposite), it is the whole experience, rather than just the waves, that has kept Josh Mulcoy coming back to Alaska. That said, the chance discovery of this perfect A-frame certainly puts the icing on the cake (following spread).

What You Need to Know

Level:
Beginner to expert.

Best time to visit:
Waves break year-round, but September offers the best chance of scoring classic conditions.

What to bring:
A warm and waterproof jacket! Temperatures rarely climb above 55 °F (13 °C) in this part of Alaska, and it rains or snows 240 days of the year.

What to do when it's flat:
Take a tour of one of the region's glaciers, or go sea kayaking in a fjord.

Fun fact:
At various times a hotbed for gold mining, timber milling, and the fur trade, nowadays fishing is the main economic driver of Mulcoy's unnamed town.

The plus to surf:
i. Aleutian Islands; ii. Sitka

ALASKA

Gulf of Alaska

CANADA

ALEUTIAN ISLANDS

NORTH PACIFIC OCEAN

UNITED STATES

Central and South America

1 *Puerto Escondido, Mexico*
2 *Nayarit, Mexico*
3 *Nosara, Costa Rica*
4 *Bocas del Toro, Panama*
5 *Cuba*
6 *Chicama, Peru*
7 *Pichilemu, Chile*
8 *Easter Island, Chile*

8

EASTER ISLAND (CHILE)

SOUTH PACIFIC OCEAN

MEXICO

Gulf of Mexico

NORTH ATLANTIC OCEAN

CUBA

5

2

BELIZE

GUATEMALA

HONDURAS

Caribbean Sea

EL SALVADOR

NICARAGUA

1

4

COSTA RICA

PANAMA

VENEZUELA

GUYANA

3

SURINAME

FRENCH GUIANA

COLOMBIA

GALAPAGOS ISLANDS

ECUADOR

BRAZIL

6

PERU

BOLIVIA

PARAGUAY

CHILE

URUGUAY

7

ARGENTINA

FALKLAND ISLANDS

Welcome to the Merciless Mex Pipe

Puerto Escondido, Mexico

As Pipeline's star rose throughout the 1970s, surfers became obsessed with finding her look-alikes around the world. Of all the waves subsequently awarded the accolade, Playa Zicatela in Puerto Escondido, Oaxaca, is surely the most deserving.

The wave quality owes to a deep offshore trench that magnifies solid Pacific swells into barrels big enough to park a bus in. Where Pipeline breaks with relative uniformity over a patch of reef, Zicatela is a beach break, prone to all the treacherous rips, shifting peaks, and closeouts that giant waves over a sand bottom often entail. Throw in the buffet of terrestrial hazards, including mosquitos, floods, and intense heat, and you've got a destination best suited to expert surfers with a penchant for the unruly.

First wrangled at size by visiting Americans in the early 1970s, locals quickly took up the mantle, establishing a formidable presence in the lineup in the decades that followed. Among the first generation was Angel "El Conejo" Salinas—one of six surfing brothers—who dreamed of becoming a famous wrestler until he discovered the even dicier thrills offered by the waves on his doorstep. Into the early 2000s, he could still be found in the lineup, often combining his passions by packing big barrels in a Mexican wrestling mask. Since then, the spot has continued to attract a similarly gung-ho breed, playing host to numerous historic rides and momentous events, including Latin America's first-ever women's big-wave competition in 2018.

The fact the beach is too dangerous for casual bathers has prevented the town from developing into one of the full-blown chain-hotel-and-golf-course tourist resorts found elsewhere in the country. But there are plenty of charming places to stay right on the beach, all offering great sea views and, a few, rattling windows that alert you to the arrival of a big swell before you've even left your bed. ～

When it comes to getting in, timing is everything. Surfers wait patiently for a break between the waves, then hop into one of the lightning-fast rip currents for a free lift to the peak (below). Local charger Quetzal Estrada (above) showing how it's done. Every year, the lifeguards perform around 800 rescues on Puerto Escondido's two main beaches alone (opposite).

What You Need to Know

Level:
Expert.

When to visit:
The biggest swells hit during the rainy season, between May and October.

What to bring:
If you're planning to surf the bigger days, breaking a board is highly likely, so it's a good idea to bring a few.

What to do when it's flat:
Sample the wild nightlife in town or go swimming with bioluminescent plankton in the Manialtepec Lagoon.

Local tip:
Although Zicatela is the main event, there are other softer waves nearby, including La Punta to the south of the town and Carrizalillo to the north.

The plus to surf:
i. West Guerrero, Mexico; ii. Guatemala

A Shangri-La for the Easy-Going Glider

*Nayarit,
Mexico*

Occupying a small chunk of Mexico's Pacific coast, the state of Nayarit is host to a bonanza of mellow setups, including point breaks, river mouths, and offshore island peaks.

Surfers have been visiting since the 1960s, historically fixated on the long rights of Matanchen Bay and Punta Mita, known as the Mexican Malibu. More recently, the region's heart has moved to Sayulita, where cobblestone streets lined with color-ful houses lead down to a playful beach-reef setup. Most days you'll find local luminary Lola Mignot there, dancing elegantly down the line on her log.

Raised on a sailboat traversing the globe, her family settled in the town in 2002 and opened one of its first boutique hotels soon after. Since then, the mix of easy rollers and laid-back living has seen Sayulita become a favorite with traveling longboarders, who flock throughout the dry season, but especially during the annual Mexi Log Fest.

The event is the brainchild of Israel Preciado, a surfer from Mexico City. As a teenager, he aspired to compete internationally but, after being denied a U.S. visa, he resolved instead to bring the longboarding world to him. In 2015, he auctioned off his quiver of surfboards to raise the funds needed to hold his first Log Fest in Sayulita. The goal was to share the unique surf culture of his homeland with the global community while providing inspiration for the next generation of local surfers. The rootsy feel resonated, and the event has grown steadily over the years, routinely attracting the globe's best male and female loggers, who compete for equal prize money alongside the talented local crop. After a few years down the coast at La Saladita, the event is back in its birthplace for 2022, where it's plain to see Preciado's founding vision has come thoroughly to fruition. Once the heats are wrapped, attendees can be found throughout the town sharing beers, exchanging ideas, and reveling in the sky-high vibes long into the night. ∼

Local Brenda Flores shares a wave with Hawaii-based slider Nique Miller during the annual Mexi Log Fest (previous spread, right). Lola Mignot is Sayulita's surfing queen, celebrated the world over for her supreme style and finesse (opposite). The town's main beach is ideally suited to longboarders, with mellow rights off a rocky point and faster, steeper lefts in the river mouth (above).

While the town offers fun waves, it also serves as a great base from which to explore the rest of the region's abundance of quality breaks, like those around Punta Mita, where a series of beaches and points dot every edge of a large headland. Here, Hayden Korte-Moore enjoys a golden-hour session in the area (below). Brenda Flores in Sayulita (opposite).

What You Need to Know

Level:
Beginner to expert.

When to visit:
For warm weather, warm water, and consistent, clean waves in the chest-high range, go from November to March.

What to bring:
Your favorite longboard, fish or mid-length, and a swimsuit.

What to do when it's flat:
Go sailing, snorkeling, and horseback riding, or visit the local farmers' market, Mercado del Pueblo.

Local tip:
In Sayulita, you can rent golf buggies by the day to get around!

The plus to surf:
i. Central Baja; ii. Los Cabos

Style Is Everything: The Art of Surfing

Style is a surfer's personal expression of the wave riding experience. It's what happens when the craftsmanship of a board shaper meets the athleticism and artistry of a surfer drawing lines on the ever-changing canvas of a breaking wave.

BY LILY PLUME

A Perennial Fascination

A lot has changed since the birth of modern surfing.
Boards have grown and shrunk in size. Subcultures
have sprouted. Performance limits have been
pushed as more monstrous waves are mastered.
Some surf breaks have even disappeared as a result
of natural disasters and coastal development.
Others have appeared in the wake of a changing
landscape. But the one thing that has remained
consistent throughout surfing's colorful history
is a shared reverence for, and obsession with, style.

To the uninitiated, the words "surf style"
might mean neoprene bikinis, tie-dye tees, and aloha
shirts. But the kind of steez we're talking about
is not something you'll see splashed across the
pages of *Vogue* (unless you count all-time style icon
Stephanie Gilmore's appearance in the magazine
in 2012). In surfing, style refers to how someone
looks on a wave, not by their choice of surfwear
but by their approach. Equal parts technical skill
and creative flair, style brings a striking element
of individuality to surfing that sets it apart from
other sports. There are only so many ways you can
shoot hoops or swing a golf club; the approaches
to surfing a wave are infinite.

The Birth of Style

From body shape and stature to board preferences
and personality, a surfer's style hinges on many
different factors. To watch the swooping bottom
turns, slack-armed trimming, and open-hearted
high lines of Australian freesurfer Torren Martyn on
a mid-length is to be mesmerized by his fluidity and
flow. Long-limbed and 6 feet, 2 inches (1.87 meters),
his straight-back poise and wide wingspan bring
a lightness to his posture and a spaciousness to
his surfing. Elsewhere on the spectrum, heavyset
Brazilian champion and Olympic gold medalist
Ítalo Ferreira on a high-performance thruster
radiates high-energy audacity, with explosive top
turns and radical aerials; a more vertical style of →

211

→ surfing. Both men are able-bodied and highly experienced in the water, but their different builds, boards, and motivations for surfing translate to different maneuvers, lines, and flourishes on a wave.

What is deemed "good" style in surfing often manifests in the placement of hands, feet, knees, and shoulders, perhaps a "hula-influenced carryover from surfing's Polynesian beginnings," as surf historian Matt Warshaw notes in his book, *The History of Surfing*. But the most widely-revered stylistic ideals that are still valued by the surfing community today have been shaped by more recent history: the culture-defining characters and early style icons of surfing's golden age.

From the classic postwar longboarding style of the late 1950s and early 1960s, epitomized in Bruce Brown's definitive surf movie *The Endless Summer* and the jazzy spontaneity of California's original power surfer Phil Edwards, to the loud and radical late-1960s shortboard revolution that paved the way to the high-performance surfing we now see on the WSL Championship Tour, this was an era of experimentation, exploration, and reinvention in all areas of wave riding. And style was everything.

A State of Flow

Hawaiian surfing legend Larry Bertlemann put it best when he said in a 1979 interview: "There's a difference between surfing and riding a wave. There's a lot of people that can ride a wave, but not many people can surf one." With a go-for-it attitude and too-cool-for-you steez, the aerial trailblazer translated his skateboarding expertise to his exploits in the water, stretching performance parameters and setting a new standard for style in the process. He took his center of gravity lower and launched his board higher than any before; his torso-twisting technique practically reinvented the turn.

While Bertlemann was making his stand-out performances at Pipeline (occasionally sporting a pair of custom-made bell-bottoms in the lineup), fellow Hawaiian Gerry Lopez was seeking oneness with the spray-spitting tubes, attempting to disappear into them completely. After making the impossibly steep drop and immediately tucking under the curl in one neat and fluid movement, he would emerge from the barrel, slender and serene, with a tai chi stare and the hint of a smile rippling across his face. Lopez arguably set the precedent for the enviable feat of making the difficult and dangerous look utterly effortless.

This effortless ease has become a hallmark of style beyond the realm of tube riding, identified by a sense of flow that animates the space between movements. How a surfer weaves together a sequence of maneuvers is as much a testament to their style and skill as the maneuvers themselves. Their interpretation of this empty space, the notes they decide to strike in those quiet moments of pause and anticipation, give subtle resonance to the climactic maneuvers.

Three-time world champion Tom Curren is a maestro of flow. His unmistakable style stems from his seamless blending of each turn into the next, drawing one long, clean, and continuous line punctuated by fierce compression and release. While his driving cutbacks and signature "double-pump" bottom turn exude a deceptive power for his relatively small stature, his posture speaks of grace: dropped back knee, tall spine, lowered arms, hovering hands.

Grace Meets The Glide

An exciting area of surfing where grace meets the glide like nowhere else in the sport is women's longboarding. Opening the "Lady Slide" segment of the celebrated film *Sprout*, a slowed-down ode to the ocean experience and alternative surf-craft, filmmaker Thomas Campbell's voiceover muses: "It's a rare occurrence when you see a woman riding a proper single fin longboard. But when you do, and it's done right, it's one of the most beautiful forms of surfing there is." Campbell was right about one thing: a woman riding a longboard is an objectively beautiful thing. You only have to share a lineup with one such lady slider to feel the magnetism of her grace, to see all eyes transfixed by this goddess-like figure gliding down the line with her toes over the nose, shucked hips, and stacked knees; the epitome of poise in a gravity-defying perch.

Released in the middle of the "retro movement," where shapers and surfers harked back to the soul-surfing '70s to reconnect with the fun of surfing, Campbell's early films—first *The Seedling* (1999) and then *Sprout* (2004)—sparked something of a renaissance in traditional longboarding. Two graceful goofy-footers were leading the way for the women: Californian Kassia Meador and Australian Belinda Baggs, who embodied the stylish feet-together, hips-forward hang-ten stance that so beautifully complements the natural curves of the feminine form.

With feature roles in both films, Meador shaped a new understanding of what women's surfing could be. "In the early 2000s, every aspiring young female longboarder had a poster of Kassia Meador on her wall," notes professional surfer Lauren Hill in *She Surf: The Rise of Female Surfing*. "Kassia helped to inspire a whole generation of young women to surf differently. She was then, as she is now, a beacon of style and grace on land and in the water."

As a result, almost two decades on, Campbell's earlier statement in *Sprout* is now only partly true—and thankfully so. Since Meador and Baggs glided into the fold of mainstream surf media, it's no longer such a rare occurrence to witness the blinding beauty of a woman riding a longboard, and riding it well. From Josie Prendergast's gentle touch and unhurried elegance in Byron Bay, to Brazilian longboarder Chloé Calmon's critical nose-riding and competitive drive and Lola Mignot's levitating hang tens in Mexico, the explosion of new talent in women's longboarding over the last decade is enough to take it toward a subculture in and of itself.

The Yin, The Yang and The Space Between

All of these women embody a grace that has long been revered in the art of wave riding, so much so that it is embedded in the legends and lore of ancient Hawaii, the birthplace of surfing. The archetypal stylings of women are woven into the rich tapestry of this early surfing culture, mythologized for their ethereal elegance on the waves. To surf like a woman was a noble feat, as illustrated by the ancient Hawaiian chant *He'e wahine ka lani* (the chief was surfing as gracefully as a woman).

Gerry Lopez echoed this sentiment when he described Honolulu-born competitive surfer Joey Hamasaki as surfing "with a poise and grace that seemed to epitomize Hawaiian surfing style." Yet Hamasaki's other contemporaries have praised her for merging this softer touch with powerful and assertive turns, producing a fluid style of surfing that cannot be labeled.

It's an anatomical fact that men and women surf differently. The contrasting weight distributions and proportions of the male and female body influence how a man or woman approaches and moves across a wave. For example, by physiological average, men have broader shoulders, helping →

The archetypal stylings of women are woven into the rich tapestry of this early surfing culture, mythologized for their ethereal elegance on the waves.

Byron-based Filipina
Josie Prendergast
epitomizes a beautifully
minimalist approach to
surfing, where the desire
to flow elegantly with
the wave trumps that of
seeking to dominate it
with maneuvers.

→ them to swivel their upper body more quickly for more powerful turns. Women typically have wider hips, meaning their surfing comes more from the rotation of their hips, working with the force of the wave to find power and speed.

Beyond these anatomical differences, there have always been gendered ideas around style in surfing. The characteristics of high-performance surfing—thrashing turns, speedy sections, and explosive aerials—are typically seen as "masculine," while the softer, slower approach and dance-like cross-stepping in traditional longboarding is deemed "feminine." But these already limiting social constructs lack the nuance and subtleties that exist in the many styles of surfing. How can something so inherently fluid be bound to such rigid parameters?

The most stylish surfers are arguably those who seamlessly blend qualities of both, a feat that seven-time world champion Stephanie Gilmore has perfected to a fine art. "I don't think she's matched by any man or woman when it comes to blending beauty, grace, and power with technicality," says Leah Dawson, a leading freesurfer and style icon with her own creative and intuitive approach to surfing. "Gilmore is in a league of her own. That inspires my surfing because she cherishes the moments of gliding, freedom, and flight, but also is able to bring that into the most ripping carve ever."

Chasing Sensations

Whether it's the smooth and soulful grace of an effortless highline glide, or the speed, power, and projection of a deep bottom turn, every surfer has their own sensations to chase in this ephemeral dance between two bodies of water. It's this pursuit of sensation that produces stylish surfing. Perhaps the most impressive feature of Gilmore's style is not a feature at all but a feeling. It's the effervescent joy that seems to bubble up inside of her and explode outwards as timeless, effortless, unparalleled style, reminding us of the simple pleasure and ineffable bliss of surfing a wave. ⌒

Off the Beaten Track in Costa Rica

Nosara,
Costa Rica

In surfing's modern epoch, Costa Rica has become the destination of choice for travelers seeking user-friendly waves in beautiful surroundings.

In the north of the country, Guanacaste province remains a firm favorite, with Tamarindo as its centerpiece. While that town has become an all-out tourist resort, replete with nightclubs and high-rise hotels, two hours south, the small district of Nosara has taken a decidedly different tack.

Since the 1970s, efforts have been made to limit development, reforest parts of the landscape previously cleared for ranching, and protect the natural ecology. Accordingly, despite a steady inflow of surfers and expats, the place has retained much of its rustic charm over the decades. First laid in 1979, the road to the main beach remains unpaved and local law prohibits any construction near the shoreline to avoid disturbing the turtles that nest there. In town, there are no chain fast-food joints but plenty of organic eateries and yoga studios. For your average surfer, the waves are something close to perfect—offshore every morning, often glassy throughout the day, and some of the most consistent in the whole of Costa Rica.

Options include the black sands of Playa Ostional, where fun rights spin off a rocky outcrop, the beginner-friendly Playa Nosara, and the excellent Playa Guiones, which offers lots of room, long walls, and the chance for tubes at low tide.

The town's promotion as a surf and yoga retreat has seen visitor numbers swell in recent years, with the pandemic's work-from-anywhere legacy bringing in a whole new wave of residents. While Nosarians have lived in relative harmony with expats for decades, there are fears that locals may be pushed out by the recent surge in prices and the delicate ecology impacted by increased footfall. However, there's hope that through community conservation efforts, already well supported by resident surfers, the newcomers will lend further weight to preserving the essence of this remote surfer's paradise for generations to come. ～

At Playa Guiones, local regulation ensures the shoreline remains completely undeveloped, preserving the charm that first drew travelers in the 1970s (previous spread). The allure of the waves also remains much the same, with long peeling walls perfect for carves, as exhibited here by Jessie Carnes (above and below).

Asher King tucks into a mini-tube at Playa Guiones (above). The trees around Nosara are teeming with wildlife. On a standard walk to the beach, you might spot several species of monkeys (including howlers, which you'll almost certainly hear before you see), white-nosed coatis, toucans, and green iguanas (opposite).

What You Need to Know

Level:
Beginner to expert.

Best time to visit:
There are waves all year round, but for dry weather, offshores, and consistent swells in the waist- to head-high range, go from December to April.

What to bring:
Your favorite shortboard and a fish, longboard, or mid-length for the smaller days.

What to do when it's flat:
Explore the region's abundant biodiversity on a guided river tour.

Local tip:
Keen to give back? Volunteer to help with local turtle conservation efforts, or get involved with one of the regular beach cleans on Playa Guiones.

The plus to surf:
i. Santa Teresa Area; ii. South Nicaragua

Panama's Lush Caribbean Archipelago

*Bocas del Toro,
Panama*

Bocas del Toro is a small archipelago lying just off Panama's northeast coast, comprising dozens of islands bejeweled with reefs, mangroves, and rainforests.

Although edged by the Caribbean, it receives consistent waves during the winter months, when fierce winds whip up jumbled but sizable swell. Historically, it was Panama's Pacific coast that captured the attention of traveling surfers, leaving the abundant potential of Bocas to be enjoyed almost exclusively by locals. But once it hit the global surf radar, it quickly became popular, and today welcomes legions of visitors ranging from backpackers to international pros.

While the islands are home to a few beach breaks, points, and playful reefs suited to intermediates, most head to Bocas for the promise of thumping barrels. And when a swell hits, there are plenty to choose from. On the main island of Colón, Bluff Beach hosts sandy drainers right on the shore, with steep drops, lightning sections, and lots of closeouts demanding full commitment. Just down the coast, Dumpers is an equally challenging affair, offering square lefts ending on shallow reef. Further south, you'll find the popular peaks of Paunch, with short punchy rights and longer whackable lefts.

Hop in one of the ubiquitous water taxis to check out the left point on the island of Careñeros, or motor over to Bastimentos for Bocas' main event: the mighty Silverbacks—a rogue thick-lipped goliath, breaking on a remote coral-encrusted outcrop. Deemed one of the heaviest slabs in the Northern Hemisphere, the shifting peaks and strong currents make it tough for even the world's best barrel wranglers. Legend has it that three-time world champ Tom Curren once tried to bodysurf a wave here and was promptly washed up on the edge of the jungle.

Luckily, the vibrant nightlife of Bocas Town and the dozen or so more palatable options nearby provide the casual surfer with plenty of ways to sample the archipelago's thrills without the need for their own date with destiny on the Silverbacks slab. ⌁

223

Hawaiian hellman Billy Kemper takes to a heaving Silverbacks barrel with aplomb (below). With many of the island's colorful dwellings built right on the water, boats remain the primary mode of transport for both locals and visitors. Most travelers begin their trip in Bocas Town, where the ubiquitous water taxis offer a great way to explore the rest of the archipelago (opposite).

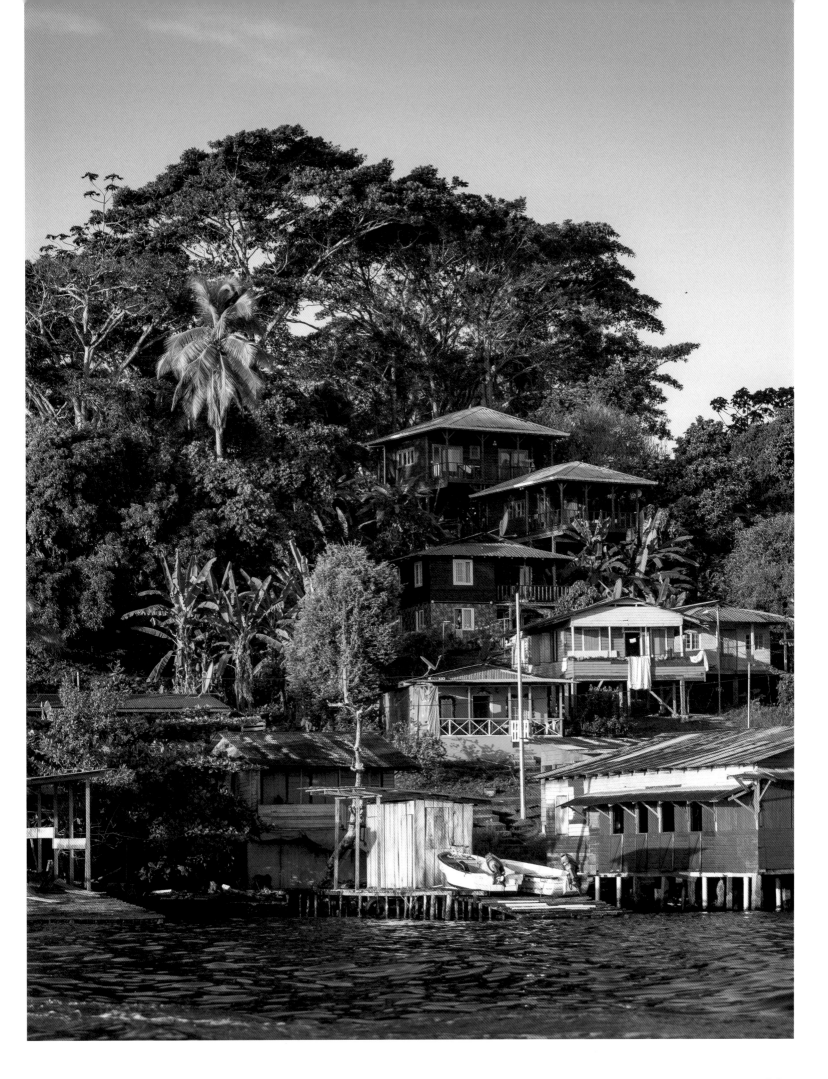

Bocas' beach breaks present a veritable playground for the high-performance surfer, offering big caverns on solid swells and fun-sized ramps on smaller ones. Here, Billy Kemper samples the former (opposite) and Nathan Florence the latter (above). The local kids are equally enthusiastic when it comes to aerial acrobatics (below).

What You Need to Know

Level:
Intermediate to advanced.

Best time to visit:
The main season runs from December to March, but there's another window from June to August known as the mini-season.

What to bring:
Binoculars for sloth spotting.

What to do when it's flat:
Take a trip to one of the beautiful outer islets for snorkeling and jungle hikes.

Fun fact:
With coral reefs abutting lowland tropical rainforest, Bocas del Toro is one of the most biologically diverse places on the planet—which is why some call it the "Galapagos of the Caribbean."

The plus to surf:
i. Panama City Area; ii. Limon, Costa Rica

Cuban Surfers Fight for Freedom

Cuba

Stretched across the meeting point of the Caribbean Sea, the Gulf of Mexico, and the North Atlantic, Cuba is an island pregnant with surf potential. But for much of its history, the fledgling local crew has been hindered by strict regulation. Following the hardships of the Cold War era, many citizens attempted to flee the country on small watercraft, leading to a government ban on entering the sea. Until recently, if caught paddling out, surfers would have their boards confiscated—a nightmare scenario against a backdrop of trade embargos that made importing a new one nearly impossible. Since the late '80s, industrious locals have had to make do, recycling boards left behind by visitors and shaping their own out of whatever they could find. For many, that was refrigerator foam, hewn with a cheese grater and finished with a heavy layer of boat resin.

That was the story that first caught the eye of the team at Makewild, a group of filmmakers from California, who traveled to the country in 2016 to meet the community and document their campaign to legitimize surfing in the eyes of their government.

The journey began in Havana, where most of Cuba's 100 or so surfers reside. Among a counter-cultural brood, the filmmakers found two passionate guides: Frank González Guerra, owner of Cuba's only shaping outfit, and Yaya Guerrero, a sea lion trainer at the local aquarium and one of the country's first female surfers.

The breaks within the city are fickle, often messy, and feature reefs so painfully sharp some require improvised boots made of beer cans just to get to the water's edge. However, few resident surfers have the means to get out and explore the rest of the country's 3,570 miles (5,745 kilometers) of coastline.

When Guerra, Guerrero, and the Makewild team set off to do just that, they discovered overcoming obstacles remained a defining feature of the surf experience. In the north, they found coastal access restricted by exclusive tourist resorts. In the southeast, near the infamous prison at Guantanamo Bay, they were hurried along by guards and told not to take any pictures. Before leaving, they stopped to observe a pumping right-hand point break from a bluff but thought better of paddling out. "That moment seemed to exemplify surfing as a whole there," says Corey McLean, director at Makewild. "The political tension, the restriction, and the forbidden fruit."

Elsewhere, they found more accessible breaks that fulfilled their visions of virgin discovery. But for Guerra and Guerrero, whether it was glassy A-frames or brown onshore dribble, they were just as quick to get out there. "When you live in a society that operates under such tight restrictions, with limited options of how to be, surf takes on a hugely therapeutic role," says McLean. "In established surf destinations, people often gripe about it being too crowded, too full of kooks, but forget to appreciate how lucky they are just to have the ease and freedom to surf at all." ∼

After traveling the length and breadth of the country, Guerra, Guerrero, and the Makewild team concluded that the beautiful south coast is where Cuba's potential as a surf destination truly lies (previous spread, left). While the waves around Havana are often messy, every dog has its day. Here, Guerra revels in classic conditions at his local (opposite).

Through her job at Havana's aquarium, Yaya Guerrero (above) was able to regularly access the internet at a time when few Cubans could. This allowed her to help coordinate and distribute surfboards donated by tourists and eventually take a central role in the campaign for the sport's advancement within the country.

What You Need to Know

Level:
Beginner to expert.

When to visit:
*For warm water, hot weather, and consistent swell,
go between November and March.*

What to do when it's flat:
*Go clubbing in a cave at Disco Ayala, or brush up
on your history in Havana's Museo de la Revolución.*

What to bring:
*With even basic medical supplies still hard to come by,
a well-stocked first aid kit is a must.*

Local tip:
*Learn about the local taxi system, governed by elaborate
hand signals, to traverse the streets of Havana like a local.*

The plus to surf:
i. East Jamaica; ii. North Coast of the Dominican Republic

A Faithful Quest for Peru's Endless Left

Chicama,
Peru

Located in northern Peru, Chicama is widely heralded as the world's longest wave, offering mind-bending rides of up to five minutes on its best days.

Peruvian fisherfolk have been gliding ashore on reed bundles, known as caballitos, for thousands of years, leading some to theorize that it was they, rather than the Hawaiians, that laid surfing's earliest foundations. Either way, it was most certainly a Hawaiian who first identified the potential of Chicama's endless peelers.

While flying out of Peru following a surf event in 1966, Chuck Shipman spotted what looked like a perfect wave from the window of his plane. He'd made good friends with a local surfer named Carlos Barreda during his stay and when he touched down, immediately wrote to him to relay what he'd seen. He included a sketch, a vague location, and an emphatic appeal to go and find it. Soon after, Barreda piled five of his buddies into a Citroen 2CV and a VW Beetle and hit the road. They scoured the coast, decamping often to push the cars over steep sandy brows and ask locals if they knew of a bay that matched the description. Finally, in Paiján their inquiries bore fruit, with news of a promising-sounding point just out of town.

After bumping along for another 30 minutes, they spotted it. Corduroy stacked to the horizon. Waves reeling off as far as the eye could see, lifted by a light offshore wind. Euphoric howls erupted from the cars. "When the screaming finally stopped," recalls Barreda, "we waxed our boards and launched ourselves into those dreamy waves."

For decades after, visiting surfers would camp or stay with local fisherfolk, but today the point houses everything from basic rooms to boutique hotels. Out in the lineup, the wave's length means you rarely have to battle to get one, especially since half the pack is usually on the long walk back up the point—or in the cavalry of motorboats there to whisk you to the peak when your shoulders and legs can take the burn no more. ～

235

Chicama is so long that it is broken into sections: El Cape, Keys, El Point, and El Hombre. Each offers a variety of fast, sucky, sometimes hollow sections and more mellow tapering walls. The final stretch, El Hombre, provides the best chance of barrels as it races over a jumble of sand and rocks towards the town pier, where the 2.5-mile (4-kilometer) point finally ends (above).

What You Need to Know

Level:
Beginner to expert.

Best time to visit:
Waves are most consistent during the dry season: April to October.

What to bring:
Maximize your rides with a board that has plenty of paddle power and enough float to get you through the soft sections.

What to do when it's flat:
Take a few days to drive up into the foothills of the Andes, and visit the pre-Inca ruins at Marcahuamachuco.

Local tip:
Chicama features four distinct sections, which only link up on rare overhead days. However, each is a great wave in its own right.

The plus to surf:
i. South Piura; ii. Ancash

Land of the Left

Pichilemu,
Chile

Around 125 miles (201 kilometers) from Santiago, near the center of Chile's surf-drenched coast, lies the surf town of Pichilemu, known as the Chilean surf capital. Here, Pacific Ocean swells roll unimpeded toward a coastline of impressive variety, offering surfers every wave imaginable. Despite this, Chile remains a somewhat low-key surf destination, possibly as a result of the daunting expanse of coast. There are literally thousands of miles of coastline in Chile and surely many waves that break empty and perfect every day, particularly in the more remote southern areas of the country.

Punta de Lobos—meaning "point of the wolves"—is the most famous wave in the area and now a designated World Surfing Reserve. It's a left-hand point break (typical of Chile), which can hold waves of 20 feet (6 meters) or more. When smaller it can offer up barrels and long walls that run all the way from the rocky point to the black-sand shore.

Ramón Navarro is the most recognized surfer from the region, thanks not just to his skill in big waves but his activism on land, which has preserved the future of Punta de Lobos. Navarro is the son of a local fisherman, and in 2013, he discovered that the 4.5-acre (.4-hectare) property on the point at Punta de Lobos was for sale, attracting the attention of developers. Worried that both the wave and the traditional fishing culture of his youth would be lost, Navarro fronted a campaign to save the area which raised enough money to purchase the property, ensuring that surfing and fishing cultures remain protected for the good of the local community.

In 2020, a further 10,000 acres (4,047 hectares) of the central Chilean coast was designated for protection in an area now known as the Piedra del Viento Coastal Marine Sanctuary. This sanctuary protects the rich species diversity of the area as well as traditional cultures and communities. The protection took surfing into account as a valuable resource, and includes the preservation of several quality waves, ensuring that Chile's land of lefts will remain unspoiled for years to come. ⌒

Punta de Lobos, in all its raw and untouched glory (previous spread, left), and Ramón Navarro (previous spread, right), the man who fought so hard to preserve it. Leon Vicuña, in one of the cold, blue left-hand tubes that characterize the region (above). Fellow local charger Cristian Merello, illuminated between rock and folding lip (opposite).

What You Need to Know

Level:
Beginner to expert.

Best time to visit:
Anytime really, Chile is incredibly consistent for waves. As with most spots, it'll be bigger on average during winter–April to September.

What to bring:
A solid backhand game if you're regular, and a readiness to smash out some of the best forehand waves of your life if you're goofy.

What to do when it's flat:
Chile's coast is populated by fishing villages that have changed little in generations. See what it's all about, and go fishing or diving for mollusks.

Local tip:
The water can be cold–in big-wave season you're looking at an average water temperature of 55 °F (13 °C).

The plus to surf:
i. Coquimbo Area; ii. Bío Bío

Following Surfing's Ancient Throughline

Easter Island,
Chile

Easter Island, also known as Rapa Nui, is the world's most isolated inhabited island, sitting 1,297 miles (2,087 kilometers) away from the nearest livable landmass, way out in the South Pacific.

It's home to the famous Moai stone statues, carved out of volcanic rock by the Indigenous Polynesians over 500 years ago. These same residents had a well-established wave riding culture, originally based around bodysurfing and later using reed bundles or planks of wood, reportedly in imitation of the turtles they saw gliding in on the shore break. They called the practice *haka-honu* (becoming the turtle) a term that appears frequently in ancient poems and chants.

Reeds and timber remained the only wave riding tools until a stroke of serendipity in the mid-1960s gifted the people their very first modern surf craft. One evening, a local fisherman named Kia Pakarati was packing up for the day when he spotted a surfboard—now thought to have fallen from a passing ship—floating toward the rocks. After diving in to retrieve it, he rode it for many years, passing it around the community until it became too waterlogged to float.

In the decades that followed, traveling surfers began visiting the island, mapping its waves, and sharing their boards with the surf-loving locals. Since the early 2000s, it's been a favorite destination of Chilean charger Ramón Navarro, who's made the five-and-a-half-hour hop from the mainland on multiple occasions. His most memorable trip came in 2013 when he finally scored a perilously fickle left he'd had his eye on for years, describing it as "only comparable to Cloudbreak."

Nowadays, the island hosts a lively collective of resident and visiting surfers, who spread out across more than a dozen reef breaks. Beginners can even book a lesson with local legend Mai Teao, who will push them into the same crystal-blue rollers of Pea Beach where the island's first surfers set out to imitate the turtles all those centuries ago. ◞

Ramón Navarro and Gabriel Villarán observe a secluded point break that, according to Navarro, hosts waves comparable to Cloudbreak in Fiji on its day (below). While most of the coastline is made up of rocky bays and headlands, there are a few sand beaches. The largest is Anakena, in the northeast of the island (opposite), while Pea Beach in the southwest offers the most learner-friendly waves.

Archeologists have discovered over 850 meticulously carved Moai statues dotted around the island. They are thought to have been carved at least 500 years ago, although some suspect they are much older (above). As with most volcanic surf destinations, the power of the waves paired with the sharp lava rocks make entry and exit from the lineup an enduring challenge (below).

What You Need to Know

Level:
Beginner to expert.

Best time to visit:
Swell arrives all year round with variable winds. For consistent overhead waves under sunny skies, book a trip for January or February.

What to bring:
A thick leg rope, your favorite big-wave board, and a ding repair kit.

What to do when it's flat:
Take a guided tour to learn about the island's fascinating ancient history.

Fun fact:
In 1990, Rapa Nui held its first surf contest, crowning none other than Pichi Pakarati (nephew of Kia, who discovered the floating surfboard over two decades prior) as its first-ever national champ.

The plus to surf:
i. Northern Ecuador; ii. Southern Ecuador

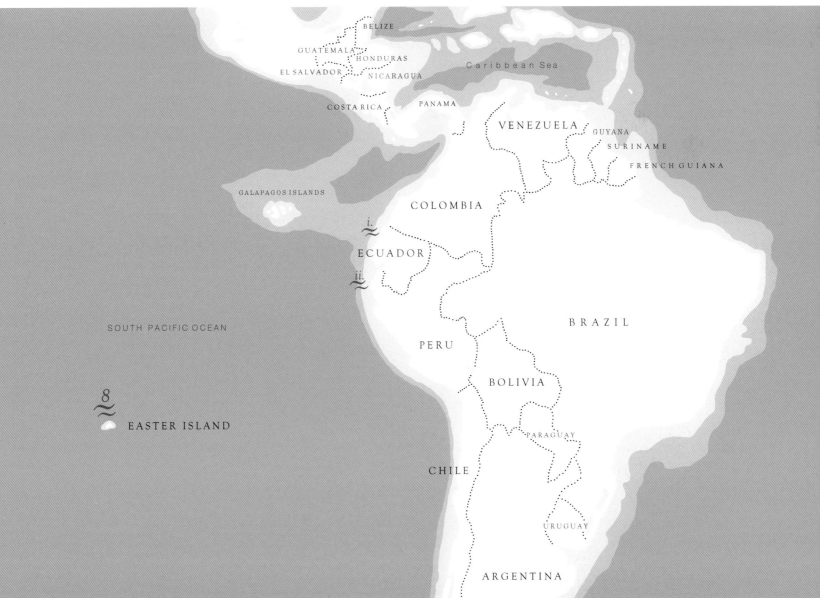

Europe

1 Nazaré, Portugal
2 Ericeira, Portugal
3 Hossegor, France
4 Cornwall, England
5 West Coast, Ireland

6 North Coast, Scotland
7 Hel Peninsula, Poland
8 The Severn Bore, England
9 Faroe Islands, Denmark
10 Lofoten Islands, Norway

NORTH ATLANTIC OCEAN

ICELAND

Norwegian Sea

10 ≈

SWEDEN

FINLAND

9 ≈
FAROE ISLANDS
(DENMARK)

NORWAY

6 ≈

ESTONIA

Baltic Sea

UNITED KINGDOM

LATVIA

LITHUANIA

5 ≈

DENMARK

7 ≈

North Sea

IRELAND

BELARUS

NETHERLANDS

8 ≈

POLAND

GERMANY

BELGIUM

4 ≈

UKRAINE

CZECHIA

SLOVAKIA

FRANCE

HUNGARY

MOLDOVA

SWITZERLAND

AUSTRIA

ROMANIA

SLOVENIA

3 ≈

CROATIA

SERBIA

BOSNIA

BULGARIA

Black Sea

ITALY

MONTENEGRO

MACEDONIA

1 ≈

ALBANIA

SPAIN

2 ≈

GREECE

TURKEY

Mediterranean Sea

PORTUGAL

CYPRUS

Europe's Sleeping Giant

Nazaré,
Portugal

For most of surfing's history, experts have said that the biggest waves on earth were to be found in the United States or Hawaii. Australia might have gotten a nod. South Africa maybe. But almost no one would have suggested a small fishing town on Portugal's Atlantic coast.

It wasn't that surfers had never found Nazaré. In fact, locals and visitors had been riding waves at Praia do Norte since the 1980s. But, in a town filled with women dressed entirely in black—in a permanent state of mourning for their husbands lost to the sea—when the waves rose to the size of buildings, surfers made plans elsewhere. And so Nazaré remained firmly off the big-wave map until one day in the early 2000s when the hunch of a local bodyboarder finally set the town on a path to surfing stardom.

253

After seeing footage of tow-in surfing in Hawaii, Dino Casimiro wondered if the aid of a jet ski might be enough to help conquer his local waves too. He took a photo of a giant day at Praia do Norte and emailed it to Hawaiian big-wave savant Garrett McNamara with an invitation to visit. Their back-and-forth lasted several years, but eventually McNamara took him up on the offer, arriving in town for the first time in 2010. Suffice to say he was astounded by what he found, and the following November the global media lit up with footage of him bouncing down the face of a 78-foot (24-meter) monster—a new world record for the biggest wave ever ridden. From there, the floodgates opened and Nazaré took its place alongside the world's foremost big-wave coliseums.

The phenomenal wave heights, which routinely reach up to five times taller than the surrounding coast, occur because of the unique shape of the seabed just offshore. The defining feature is an underwater trench—three times deeper than the Grand Canyon—that allows swells to travel unimpeded all the way to the shore. The sudden depth change forces them upwards, where they converge with swell lines refracting across the bay, creating the huge and unpredictable teepees for which the break is known.

Today, every swell sees the lineup abuzz with dozens of tow-in teams from around the world, while spectators line the cliffs for big-wave surfing's greatest spectacle. Just witnessing a wave break here is a humbling experience. It's impossible to imagine what it must be like to actually ride one. ~

Thousands of spectators line the swell-battered headland separating the town of Nazaré from Praia do Norte when a giant swell rolls in (previous spread). Unlike at regular surf spots, big waves are often happily shared by more than one rider. Here, Lucas Chumbo and Julian Reichmann drop in together (bottom, right). Justine Dupont grabs the rope as a set feathers out the back (opposite).

The unique shape of the sea bed offshore sees swells bend and converge into giant triangles as they meet the beach (above). When facing down a huge wall of white water, surfers often opt to pop up and use their board like a diving platform in order to get down as deep as possible. Here, Lucas Chumbo prepares for the plunge (opposite).

What You Need to Know

Level:
Expert.

When to visit:
For XL swells, go between November and March.

What to do when it's flat:
Visit the iconic lighthouse fort on the headland, now home to a surf museum.

What to bring:
Pro big-wave riders arrive with all sorts of gear, including jet skis, specialist big-wave boards, and inflation vests. If you're just coming to watch, a pair of binoculars and a camping chair should do it!

Fun fact:
Nazaré is one of the world's most consistent big-wave spots, with dozens of clean double-overhead and bigger days surfed each winter.

The plus to surf:
i. Porto Area; ii. Algarve

A Wave for All Seasons

Ericeira,
Portugal

A swell-rich coastline in western Portugal that soaks up all the Atlantic has to offer yet is within easy reach of a major European capital city: what more could you want? You'll find waves to suit everyone in the hundreds of miles of Portuguese coastline, but if you want great surf in a concentrated area, head to Ericeira.

Designated Europe's first World Surfing Reserve in 2011, in Ericeira your greatest challenge won't be finding waves but deciding which to surf. São Lourenço is a consistent right-hand reef that holds more swell than any other spot in the area. It transforms into a big-wave spot on larger swells, but there is a mellow inside section on smaller days

that suits less advanced surfers and longboarders. Coxos is often dubbed Portugal's (and even Europe's) best wave. It's a powerful right-hand reef break best avoided if you aren't high on confidence or crowds, but essential for advanced surfers. Up a level still are Crazy Left and Cave. Both are serious, hollow waves for expert surfers only. They were pioneered by bodyboarders who could make the critical take-offs and initially seemed off-limits to other surfers. But they're now recognized as offering some of the finest barrels in Europe and are frequented by the world's best when the World Championship Tour makes its yearly stop in Peniche just up the coast. For an indication of just how serious Cave is, John John Florence was hospitalized here as a result of lacerations and bruising after coming into contact with the reef.

Ribeira d'Ilhas is one of the more popular spots where it's still possible to get some waves due to its wide bay and multiple reefs. It's a great spot to check from the surrounding cliffs, and on good days, right-hand walls will connect the reefs from the outside all the way in, leading to long, joyous rides.

If the more advanced waves aren't applicable, you'll find lots of peaky beach breaks to hone your skills and accommodating surf camps to help you progress. ⌒

Coxos is considered the region's finest wave, serving up epic tubes and long, powerful walls (previous spread and below). Just down the coast Cave is a formidable slab, renowned for sending surfers to the hospital. Here, João Guedes sets a line as boils bubble up from the almost dry reef below (previous spread, right) and Pedro Boonman navigates a deceptively friendly-looking bowl (opposite).

What You Need to Know

Level:
Beginner to expert.

Best time to visit:
As with many European spots, September to November will offer up the best combination of warmth and waves.

What to bring:
A willingness to share the best waves or search for the quieter ones.

What to do when it's flat:
Jump off rocks and swim in secluded coves. Eat barbecued sardines that will make you wonder what those things you've been eating in cans were.

Local tip:
Rent a car. There are even more quality spots with shelter from every wind direction just a short drive away.

The plus to surf:
i. Peniche; ii. Lisbon Area

From Swamp to Silver Coast

Hossegor,
France

Southwest France's Landes region encompasses more than 60 miles (97 kilometers) of sandy coast-line, extending north from the city of Bayonne to Biscarrosse Plage. Although there are great breaks throughout, the most iconic are to be found in the small town of Hossegor. Historically a mass of dunes and boggy marshland, the town came into being in the 19th century after Napoleon III began planting pine trees to shore up the land. By the late 1960s, the medley of blue ocean, white sand, and green forest had become a favorite with holidaying Parisians and surfers from across the continent.

Home to five named beaches along a single unbroken stretch, Hossegor offers a veritable playground for wave riders of all abilities. Starting in the south, Plages Sud and Centrale serve up beginner and improver-friendly waves, with some swell protection from the nearby harbor at Capbreton. La Nord is the resident big-wave spot, with an outside bank holding waves up to triple overhead. It offers fast steep drops and occasional barrels and is always well-attended by an enthusiastic local crowd on specialist big-wave boards. Next is La Graviere, the most famous of the town's waves. On its day, it produces flawless barrels, detonating right on the shoreline in front of a Second World War-era concrete bunker that protrudes from the dunes. To the north is Les Culs Nus (the bare bottoms), the local nudist beach, which works well in smaller swells, offering a variety of different waves depending on the vagaries of the sandbanks and fast-moving tide.

Flanked by the similarly surf-rich towns of Capbreton and Seignosse, there's no shortage of options along this stretch when conditions are good. Swell arrives year-round, generally accompanied by offshore winds in the mornings and evenings. With no kinks in the coastline, however, if a succession of Atlantic storm fronts move in, the waves can be blown out for weeks. ⌐

The pack waits patiently at La Nord, rhino chasers at the ready (previous spread). Visiting Aussie Kael Walsh sends it skyward on a shore break ramp (above). Just down the beach, Hawaiian Mason Ho slips beneath a glowing green lip line (below). Evening offshores brush a solid fall swell on a glorious evening at La Graviere (opposite).

Looking south from Seignosse: beyond an expanse of deep soft sand and the bustling beachfront of Plage Centrale (above), past PV Laborde ensconced in a fine Graviere drainer, and all the way to the Pyrenees beyond (below). Despite a crackdown on free camping in recent years, Hossegor remains a favorite among traveling surfers living the van life (opposite).

What You Need to Know

Level:
Beginner to expert.

Best time to visit:
Fall serves up consistent waves accompanied by warm weather and morning offshores.

What to bring:
From October onward, you'll need a warm coat for the chilly mornings and summery attire for the balmy afternoons.

What to do when it's flat:
Enjoy a day out in the beautiful town of Biarritz, or head up into the Pyrenees.

Local tip:
The town center is packed with great restaurants and bars that come alive every night in summer and when the world tour event rolls into town.

The plus to surf:
i. Gironde; ii. La Côte Basque

ICELAND

FAROE ISLANDS

FINLAND

NORWAY

SWEDEN

ESTONIA

Baltic Sea

UNITED KINGDOM

LATVIA

DENMARK

LITHUANIA

North Sea

BELARUS

IRELAND

NETHERLANDS

POLAND

BELGIUM

GERMANY

CZECHIA

SLOVAKIA

UKRAINE

FRANCE

HUNGARY

i.

SWITZERLAND

AUSTRIA

ROMANIA

NORTH ATLANTIC OCEAN

ii.

SLOVENIA

CROATIA

SERBIA

BOSNIA

BULGARIA

ITALY

MONTENEGRO

MACEDONIA

SPAIN

ALBANIA

PORTUGAL

GREECE

Mediterranean Sea

Britain's Rugged Surfing Heartland

*Cornwall,
England*

Jutting out into the North Atlantic, Cornwall occupies mainland Britain's craggy southwest corner. With 433 miles (697 kilometers) of swell-drenched coastline, it's no surprise surfing has been popular here for over half a century, with a rich tradition of riding waves on wooden bellyboards dating back even further. The result is a diverse and well-established surf culture, with numerous distinct communities throughout the region, each with their own cast of eccentric elders, enthusiastic newcomers, and dedicated young rippers.

While known today as a tourist destination, signs of the industry on which the region was built remain etched into the coastal landscape. Old fishing harbors abut many of the best breaks, and disused engine houses, which mark the top of subterranean mine shafts, tower high on the headlands between picturesque coves. An expansive coastal path, which grants access to the entirety of Cornwall's Atlantic frontier, also nods to a bygone era, having been originally forged by smugglers and the coastguards trying to catch them. The path looms large in the contemporary surfing experience, offering the chance to scour the coastline's every nook and cranny for uncrowded waves.

Giant tidal ranges and exposure to the open ocean mean conditions change wildly, from season to season and minute to minute. In the summer, the many long sandy beaches fill up with tourists and the waves are generally small and can go flat for weeks. In the winter, a procession of storms can usher in gale-force winds and swells of 6 feet (2 meters) or more for months on end. But with spots facing every point of the compass, you can almost always find somewhere sheltered to surf, as long as you don't mind driving down narrow country lanes and hiking across wind-riven clifftops to get there. ∽

Izzy Henshall with a casual cross step at Sennen Cove (previous spread, left). With no defined swell season, great waves can roll in at any time of the year. Here, Adam Griffiths busts the mid-winter blues with a dreamy sunset session near Newquay (previous spread, right). James Parry, framed by the remnants of an old copper mine (below). Alan Stokes at the region's famous Fistral Beach (opposite).

What You Need to Know

Level:
Beginner to expert.

Best time to visit:
*With consistent swell and generally mild weather, September
and October are the best months for a surf trip.*

What to bring:
*A good all-round board that will go in anything from knee-high
to overhead waves will allow you to get in most days.*

What to do when it's flat:
*Explore hidden sea caves and go rock jumping on a guided
coasteering tour.*

Local tip:
*Sate your post-surf hunger with a Cornish pasty from
a local bakery.*

The plus to surf:
i. Swansea Area, Wales; ii. Brittany, France

The Magic Energy of the Emerald Isle

West Coast, Ireland

When considering the elements that make surfing in the North Atlantic magical, Ireland has them all in spades. Grand scenery, a rich culture of myth and storytelling, cold water, warm hospitality, and a dazzling array of exceptional waves. Surfing here is both long-lived and continually evolving. In the northwest corner alone you'll find reefs, river mouths, and points that have been surfed for five decades and a collection of intense slabs that were only pioneered in the last two.

This country's big-wave dawn began in the early 2000s when locals Richie Fitzgerald and Brit Gabe Davies were inspired by a season in Hawaii to try tow-in surfing at Mullaghmore. Despite their admission that they had no idea what they were doing in the early days—buzzing around on a jet ski that looked like something out of *Miami Vice*—the waves they rode would prove seminal to the development of the scene.

The next boom happened a little later in the decade, following the discovery of several more reefs that produced barrels as big and wide as anywhere in Europe. Chief among them was a break called Aileen's, located at the base of the Cliffs of Moher. Only accessible by sea or a hair-raising 30-minute scramble down a goat track, paddling out here typifies the Irish surf experience. Foam swirls in the high winds as waves rear up and slam onto a shallow ledge, while hundreds of meters of sheer weather-beaten cliff stare down at you from above.

Mullaghmore Head, captured from high above the lineup (previous spread, left). Andrew Cotton at the break nicknamed Prowlers (previous spread, right). Conor Maguire prepares to descend a Mullaghmore mountain (bottom, left) and waits to alight beneath the Cliffs of Moher (bottom, right). Over the last few years, young Enda Curren has become one of the top resident chargers at Mullaghmore (opposite).

The rapid progression that occurred here and at the equally mystical Riley's in the late 2000s made for a groundbreaking period in European surfing, characterized by era-defining rides, brutal injuries, and countless near-drownings.

More recently, the focus has moved back up the coast to Mullaghmore, where a close alliance of locals and expats has dedicated themselves to pushing the limits of possibility. Central to the group is firefighter Peter Conroy, who has instigated an innovative approach to big-wave safety, offering lessons to all on how to drive support jet skis and perform rescues and resuscitations. It's a marked departure from the swashbuckling attitude of yore and has transformed the break's regular surfers into a highly experienced safety crew, bonded by the solidarity that comes with repeatedly saving each other's lives.

When, in 2020, a historic swell loomed and Irish charger Conor Maguire readied for battle, other locals immediately stepped up to support his efforts. They patrolled on jet skis and spotted from the cliff while Maguire's mentor Barry Mottershead picked his waves and towed him in. Thanks to their efforts and his own prowess, Maguire was able to snag the biggest wave ever surfed on Irish shores—coming in at a whopping 60 feet (18 meters).

"There's no way I could have even gone out there if it wasn't for all my friends," he told Sea Sessions afterward. "It was a dream to have those guys there supporting me ... That felt better than any of the recognition I got in the media for sure." ～

First discovered by Cornish bodyboarder and photographer Mickey Smith in 2007, Riley's is one of Europe's most awe-inspiring heavy wave surf spots. Over the last decade and a half, waves ridden here have broken bones, defined careers, and graced dozens of magazine covers (below).

What You Need to Know

Level:
Beginner to expert.

Best time to visit:
The biggest swells usually hit between November and March, but for those not seeking XL conditions, the milder months of September and October are prime.

What to bring:
If you're going in the fall, bring gear for every possible weather condition (but especially cold and wet days).

What to do when it's flat:
Explore the tranquil coastal landscape, or head to Dublin for classic Irish craic.

Local tip:
Beyond the high-profile spots, this region is home to dozens of great breaks. Buy a local surfer a few pints of Guinness and they might just share some secrets with you.

The plus to surf:
i. Portrush Area, Northern Ireland; ii. North Coast of Scotland

Cold Consolations in Caledonia

North Coast, Scotland

Few places combine rugged rural charm and world-class reef breaks better than Scotland's north coast.

The best wave is a right-hand point called Thurso East, which peels into a peat-tinged river mouth in the shadow of a dilapidated castle. Access is easy thanks to an accommodating farmer, who lets you park right on the point next to his cowshed. Many of the region's best waves, however, require a long traipse through boggy fields. Thankfully, right-to-roam laws here mean—as long as you're respectful—you can access any part of the coast you like, adding to a sense of adventure that grows with every bend in the road.

Situated over two hours' drive from the nearest city, the coast's remoteness, combined with long flat spells and harsh winters, mean it can be a tough and lonely place to live, so there's a strong sense of community among local surfers. They turn out year-round, come sleet, rain, or shine, to ride on whatever the Atlantic has to offer. Many sessions end with a lively debrief in Thurso's recently built clubhouse, which sits overlooking the waves, between stacks of hay bales and farm machinery. Another popular option is to decant to a nearby pub and warm up in front of an open fire over a dram of the world-famous local whiskey.

Although it's mainly the many barreling reefs around Thurso that attract the surf world's attention, there are lots of beautiful sandy beaches and river mouth breaks as you head west. Crowds thin out and the scenery grows wilder, with imposing mountain ridges, huge lochs, and rocky islets pulling your gaze in every direction as you wind along the coastal road. While camper vans are the most popular accommodation choice, there are many other options for surf trippers traveling by car, bike, or even on foot. These include pubs, hostels, bed-and-breakfasts, and bothies—simple stone huts left open for weary hikers to stay in for free, and the perfect option for surfers seeking a truly spartan adventure in the Scottish wilderness. ⁓

Multiple British champion Lucy Campbell hones her slab skills beneath pastel skies one beautiful fall evening (previous spread). The A836 road runs the length of the north coast, connecting dozens of remote and rugged beaches (below). Will Bailey sits in a heavy tube at a spot named Bagpipes in honor of the country's national instrument and the wave's resemblance to Pipeline (opposite).

What You Need to Know

Level:
Intermediate to expert.

Best time to visit:
The most consistent swell season is from November to March, but with more daylight and the chance of warmer weather, September and October are also a good bet.

What to bring:
A solid pair of hiking boots and your favorite tube-riding board.

What to do when it's flat:
Explore the beautiful local surroundings or head four-and-a-half-hours' drive south to Glenshee for snowboarding in the winter months.

Local tip:
Keep an eye out for orcas and the northern lights, both of which are occasionally spotted around Thurso.

The plus to surf:
i. Outer Hebrides; ii. East Coast

The Hardcore Surfers of the Hel Peninsula

*Hel Peninsula,
Poland*

The Hel Peninsula appears like a slender finger of sand reaching from Poland's north coast into the Baltic Sea. Just 492 feet (150 meters) across at its narrowest point, the sandy terrain is covered by a blanket of dense vegetation, interrupted only by a scattering of port towns and a single road that runs all the way to its end.

The name is thought to derive from the Old Polish *hyl*, which translates as "exposed place"—and indeed, the peninsula's seaward coastline is perfectly angled to catch swells from all sides of the Baltic. A regiment of wooden groins protrude from the shoreline, trapping the fast-moving sand and creating waves with just enough consistency and ferocity to make this the epicenter of the Polish surf scene.

Surfing in a sea is an altogether different experience than surfing in an ocean. On Europe's western flank, waves are created by groundswells, generated by storms thousands of miles away, which become gradually more organized as they travel across the Atlantic. Surfers in Poland rely on intense storms much closer to home to whip up wind swell in the shallow waters of the Baltic Sea. As a result, swells are inconsistent, often short-lived, and accompanied by howling winds. Combine this with the strong rip currents that churn around the spit and the fact sea temperatures can plummet to as low as 32 °F (0 °C), and to most, surfing in Poland seems like an unattractive prospect.

But every now and again, the wind drops or swings offshore while the waves it creates still buffet the coast. These are the magical moments the surfers of Poland wait for all year, and their allure has laid the groundwork for a thriving scene on the peninsula. While fall and winter are the prime months for the country's hardcore surfers, Hel boasts plenty of amenities for the casual summer wave rider too, including surf schools, rental shops, and even an array of surf-themed cocktail bars and bistros, complete with compulsory surfboard signage. ⌒

Polish surf champ Kuba Kuzia springs off the bottom on a crisp winter morning (above). During peak swell season, there are often fun waves to be found on either side of Władysławowo Marina, with good sand build-up beneath ice-covered tetrapods on the north (below) and protection from the northwesterly wind on the south side (opposite).

What You Need to Know

Level:
Beginner to expert.

Best time to visit:
The best waves arrive throughout the fall and winter months, from November to March.

What to bring:
With water temperatures barely above freezing in the winter, a hooded 6 mm wetsuit, boots, and gloves are essential.

What to do when it's flat:
If the waves are blown out, try kitesurfing in Puck Bay, considered one of the best spots for the sport in Europe.

Fun fact:
The waters around Hel are littered with more than 1,500 shipwrecks, most of which date back to the Second World War.

The plus to surf:
i. Kaliningrad, Russia; ii. West Coast, Lithuania

The Muddy Brothers of the River Severn

*The Severn Bore,
England*

It's hard to imagine a surf experience further from the sunbaked beaches of California or Hawaii than riding waves on a cold, muddy river through the heart of the English countryside. It turns out, however, that the Severn Bore's army of devotees is as stoked as any other surf community on earth.

The bore is a single wave that forms just upriver from the city of Bristol in the southwest of England. Its creation owes to a chance convergence of tide and terrain. When the moon and sun align every few weeks, their combined gravitational pull creates a large tidal swing (known as a spring tide). As the incoming flow is forced between the Severn Estuary's narrow channel, the head of the tide forms into a wave. From there, it trundles upriver for about 21 miles (34 kilometers), breaking and reforming as it winds its way past pubs, churches, and grazing sheep.

The bore was first surfed by Colonel "Mad Jack" Churchill in the summer of 1955. A decorated military man, Churchill is best known for taking a sword and longbow into battle during the Second World War. Or he was, until the day he towed his homemade wooden surfboard behind his motorcycle to the banks of the Severn and paddled out into the history books. The wave continues to attract a similarly eccentric crew, who call themselves "The Muddy Brothers." They share a deep sense of camaraderie, born largely of the fact that, unlike in the ocean, the single wave must be shared by all. They ride shoulder to shoulder, shouting tips and encouragement to one another as they go. Following a wipeout, surfers rush back to their vehicles to race the wave upstream to the next access point. Any sort of tricks or maneuvers are generally eschewed, with a leg-achingly long ride being the ultimate goal for the seasoned bore surfer. The world record belongs to Steve King, a local railway engineer who managed to cover 7.5 miles (12 kilometers) during a single, unbroken ride that lasted over an hour. ⌒

Each year, a guide is released detailing the size, time, and date of each bore-producing tide. Here, surfers gather on the riverbank, eagerly anticipating the arrival of one of the season's biggest (opposite). Spectators watch the bore bowl by unridden at Minsterworth (above). Over a dozen surfers share a ride on a misty morning beneath Newnham church (below).

David Harber rolls the dice on a rare left-hander and is rewarded with a solo ride on a sheet-glass canvas (above). Since spring high tides are always first thing in the morning, winter bores often demand you enter the river before sunrise. Here, Dave Butterton crosses a frosty field in Arlingham one freezing January morning (below).

What You Need to Know

Level:
Intermediate to expert.

Best time to visit:
The biggest tides occur around the spring and fall equinoxes, from February to April and August to October.

What to bring:
A big board that you don't mind getting a little battered!

What to do when it's flat:
Enjoy a Sunday roast at the Severn Bore Inn in Minsterworth.

Local tip:
The village of Arlingham is the best spot for first-time bore riders; it offers plenty of space, and the opportunity to catch up with the wave further upstream if you miss it.

The plus to surf:
i. North Devon; ii. Bournemouth Area

Giants, Witches, and Wedges

Faroe Islands, Denmark

Scattered between Britain, Norway, and Iceland, the Faroe Islands comprise 18 jagged landmasses, rising from the stormy waters of the North Atlantic: a truly wild place, by any standards. For hundreds of years, the inhabitants survived on farming and fishing, living in small clusters of grass-roofed houses huddled together in broad glacial valleys. Despite its obvious swell exposure and 687 miles (1,106 kilometers) of coastline concealing all manner of reefs and sandy coves, the country's waves were only explored well into this millennium, with the first local surfers putting down roots even more recently.

It all began in 2006 when lensman Yassine Ouhilal arrived on a photo trip with a group of American surfers. After asking around, someone introduced them to a local kitesurfer named David Geyti, who, despite knowing nothing of the islands' waves, offered to show them around his home. Ouhilal ended up staying for the whole winter, mapping numerous breaks and teaching Geyti how to surf, pushing him in the shallows on a windsurfer with the sail removed. After Ouhilal left, Geyti →

Much of the Faroese coastline is inaccessible by road, meaning the hunt for waves requires plenty of hiking over snowy and mountainous terrain (top). The small village of Tjørnuvík is home to the islands' best-known and most consistent surf break, producing rights and lefts that are brushed clean by the dominant winds during most sizable storm swells (bottom, right).

→ got himself a real board shipped over from Norway and for a few years, he surfed the beaches with nothing but the sea stacks and the occasional curious seal for company. Then one day Kat Bærentsen turned up.

Born and raised in the Faroes, Bærentsen had learned to surf on a trip to Costa Rica, only discovering it was possible back home after happening upon a Facebook group set up by Geyti, inviting people to join him in the waves.

Over the years that followed, several crews of traveling pros turned up to explore the islands, with a stream of films and articles in surf magazines following in their wake. But without any lifeguards, surf schools, or rental shops, Bærentsen and Geyti remained the sole resident surfers.

Finally in 2019, amid growing interest from locals, visitors, and the country's tourism board, Bærentsen and friend Andras Brixen Vágsheyg decided to establish the islands' first proper surfing

provisions. Based out of a small shack on Tjørnuvik beach, the Faroe Islands Surf Guide now offers lessons and rentals alongside a range of other ocean activities, including snorkeling and cliff jumping—and an outdoor hot tub to warm up in afterward. Today, a small, tight-knit group of local surfers can be regularly found in the waves, almost all having fallen in love with the pastime under Bærentsen's enthusiastic tutelage. ∼

Beyond Tjørnuvík beach are two stacks, known as the witch and the giant. Legend has it that they were sent from Iceland to capture the Faroes many moons ago. After spending the night trying to wrench the land onto the giant's back, the sun rose and turned them both to stone, and there they've stood ever since (previous spread, right). The Faroes first local surfer, David Geyti (opposite).

What You Need to Know

Level:
Beginner to expert.

Best time to visit:
The main spot of Tjørnuvík needs a solid swell to wrap around the headland, so from November to February is your best chance of scoring.

What to bring:
With winter temperatures hovering around 32 °F (0 °C), a good set of thermals and a thick wetsuit are a must.

What to do when it's flat:
Visit the beautiful Múlafossur waterfall and its lively puffin colony.

Fun fact:
No matter where you are in the islands, you're never more than 3 miles (4.8 kilometers) from the coast.

The plus to surf:
i. South Coast of Iceland; ii. Hoddevik Area, Norway

Viking Treasures in the Far North

*Lofoten Islands,
Norway*

To a certain type of surfer, just looking at the Lofoten Islands in two dimensions is enough to raise the blood. This archipelago off Norway's northwest coast is exposed to fierce Arctic storms, sending swells toward a coastline with the kind of brutal, craggy geography that means an abundance of potential points and reefs ripe for discovery. The islands are uniquely mountainous, with several peaks above 3,000 feet (914 meters) rising directly from sea to summit. This ensures a wild, raw setting and perhaps the most spectacular backdrops anywhere in the world.

It's believed the Lofoten area has been settled for at least 11,000 years, but while the Vikings were certainly seafarers, the first people regularly riding waves for pleasure didn't appear until the late 1990s. For a time they were sparse—not so anymore. These local pioneers lament a recent past when Lofoten had a surf culture much like that of California in the 1950s.

Today, Unstad Beach is a globally renowned spot and has played a significant role in the rocketing popularity of cold-water surfing. A deep bay with a wide entrance faces northwest and attracts the predominant west/southwest swell. At the southern end is Unstad Left and to the north, Unstad Right. Both are quality waves that reel into the bay over bouldered points and can offer fast, hollow sections. More friendly waves break in the middle of the beach between these points.

If you've seen shots of cold-water surfing with a jagged, snow-covered peak that rises almost vertically from sea level just behind the wave, chances are you've been looking at Unstad. And those images you've seen of Mick Fanning surfing under the northern lights? That's Unstad too. Although there's no doubt that high-profile coverage has somewhat diluted the dream the images hope to portray, Unstad remains an iconic spot and a quality wave—or perhaps it's just a gateway to Lofoten secrets still to be found. ∽

Polish surfers Kuba Kuzia and Krzysztof Sikora enjoy a breathtakingly beautiful trek to the surf (previous spread). Unstad's waves were first unveiled to the world through a series of surf magazine articles and movies throughout the 1990s. Since then, the bay's snowy backdrops have become the poster child for the global cold-water surfing movement (opposite).

Lofoten is one of the best places on earth to see the magical aurora borealis—and one of the only places where you can see them twinkling above a pair of pumping point breaks (above).

What You Need to Know

Level:
Beginner to expert.

Best time to visit:
November to February will be most consistent for waves, but with very short windows of daylight. Conversely, the summer months could see you surfing nearly 24 hours a day, given waves and energy!

What to bring:
The thickest wetsuit you have and a camera to capture a melding of light and landscape unlike anywhere else—especially if you're lucky enough to catch the aurora borealis.

What to do when it's flat:
Climb a mountain. If you're into splitboarding or ski touring, then Lofoten offers some of the most stunning terrain in the world— literally summit to sea.

Local tip:
Stay warm!

The plus to surf:
i. Bodø Area; ii. Stavanger Area

Sub-Zero Surfing in the Lands of Ice and Snow

Surfing is no longer just palm trees and tropical blue waters. In some of the planet's coldest regions, hardy surfers chip ice from boards, wade through snowdrifts, and plunge into freezing oceans. Often they're alone, but many wouldn't have it any other way. It's not the original surf dream, but it might be the only one left.

BY JAMIE P. CURRIE

While the backdrop couldn't be more different from *The Endless Summer* idyll, the quest remains much the same—to find perfect waves in exotic surrounds, with not another soul in sight. Here, Josh Mulcoy strikes gold in Alaska.

A New Hope

If you ask most people to describe their ideal surf experience, it probably wouldn't involve wading through snowdrifts or shielding yourself from sleet and hail, driven by gale-force winds with piercing intent. Nor would it include cold-water-induced headaches so severe it feels as though someone is driving nails through your skull. And it likely wouldn't involve a post-surf experience that feels a little like traumatic shock. There's a certain vulnerability about being trapped in your wetsuit by numbness with no one around to help. (And even if there was, you might be too cold to form the words to ask for it.) At these times, some might question the wisdom of such exposure to the cold.

Yet, in some parts of the world, these are the realities of surfing. Some people relish it, some simply endure it, and others go so far as to chase it. Cold-water surfing is not just a geographical necessity, it's a quest to rediscover surfing as it once was: a joyful act of adventure full of empty, perfect waves. A chance to relive the golden years of surf culture in hues of icy blue.

Today, at the top of many surfers' bucket lists are places such as Scotland, Ireland, Norway, Canada, Iceland, Alaska, Russia, and even Antarctica—locations where finding new waves, or at the very least, empty ones, is still possible. Extreme conditions are found in all of these places; many face long winters with temperatures that drop to dramatic lows—fancy taking a dip in Antarctica when the weather outside is -40 °F (-40 °C). Some do. Advances in wetsuit technology, forecasting, and global travel networks mean that such cool-water places are no longer exclusively the domains of masochists, outcasts, and searchers.

313

Breaking the Ice

It's uncertain where the first surfers to brave the cold plunged in, but we do know that it predated the invention of the wetsuit. Possibly, people in Northern California were the first legitimate cold-water surfers of the pre-wetsuit era, though undoubtedly bold souls dipped cautious toes in some of the world's colder seas from the late 1920s onwards. On the Kintyre Peninsula in Scotland, anecdotal evidence suggests that people may have surfed on rudimentary boards shaped by the local undertaker as early as the 1930s. Even in the summer months, the average sea temperature there is around 55 °F (13 °C). To surf these waves with homemade boards and without wetsuits was no mean feat.

Over the course of the next two decades, people made sporadic attempts at surfing in some of the world's colder regions, but it wasn't until the late 1960s that surfing in these places began to take root. Scattered bands of surfers appeared in Scotland with boards that were homemade or brought back from warmer climates. These hardy souls surfed in shorts through gritted teeth, warmed by the idea that they could establish a California-style beach culture in the far north. Later, they donned adapted diving suits, wore wool sweaters under thin neoprene vests, and used rubber gloves intended for washing dishes, all in the quest to keep warm.

The invention of the wetsuit changed the game. From initially ill-fitting and ineffective, they have evolved to become the sleek neoprene wetsuits we see today. Available in a range of thicknesses from 1–7 mm, they come with a variety of accessories—including hoods, boots, and gloves—designed to help you stay in the water, in relative comfort, for hours at a time. Today, every major wetsuit manufacturer caters to surfers based in subzero climates, and some brands are dedicated entirely to this lifestyle.

Frozen Ideals

Cold-water surfing tends to be photogenic, which has introduced a new reason to seek out rugged isolation. In contrast to the traditional surf imagery of palm trees, white sand, and azure waters, we now have volcanic shorelines of black sand and jagged rocks, backdrops of snow-capped peaks, surfing under the midnight sun—or perhaps even beneath the flicker of the aurora borealis. Images that capture the interplay between light, water, and landscape sell both surf products and dreams. And even though the setting is different, the dream is the same as it ever was: one of perfect waves all to yourself in a land that feels like you're the first and last to be there. It's the original surf ideal flipped on its head. It's the dream of an endless winter.

Beyond the aesthetic appeal of the landscape, cold-water locations retain an essential wildness that appeals to surfers. They're generally a bit harder to get to, and they're almost certainly harder to score waves in. Though accommodations and surf camps are emerging in these new locations, you won't find luxury resorts like you would in Bali or the Maldives, and you'll likely spend a lot of time waiting for the weather to cooperate. Most places require a little more work and the understanding that it's a bit of a gamble.

The trade-off? Empty waves and the gratification of having worked for something. Warm-water locations have been mined and exhausted by surf travel and exploration. Cold-water surf spots still retain the essence of surf culture. Many surfers today will happily sacrifice comfort and company in pursuit of idealism. At its heart, surfing is about discovery. It's about taking chances and seeking moments in time that will never be repeated. These moments happen in the cold.

Cold Water, Warm Souls

Cold-water surfing isn't just for travelers and seekers looking to dip their toes in and go home, but without them perhaps many surf communities would never have been established. Surfing spreads like seeds propagated by trees. Surfers are guided by elemental forces—they are compelled to go out into the world, to explore and share their love of waves. Where they might land is anyone's guess. Often the first to surf many of the world's more remote regions were visitors who left boards behind. If, that is, they ever left themselves. Locals sometimes watched in trepidation as mysterious strangers paddled into raging seas. But then, they paddled out too, and so a new surf culture was born. If these strangers were first viewed with suspicion and curiosity, their legacy is often joy.

The value of this in some of the colder and more remote regions of the world cannot be overstated. A surfing life gives purpose, and it helps to forge connections with land and sea that are lost as people are drawn to urban centers. As surfers, we see value in places where others cannot, and this in turn may help these places to survive, with surfing becoming an unlikely catalyst for community.

Today, if you visit many of these cold-water surf locations you are likely to meet eclectic characters and locals both welcoming and memorable. By and large, many of these people may live where they do simply because of surfing and have relocated to remote regions for that specific purpose.

In scattered frozen outposts like the Faroe Islands, the Shetlands, or Siberia, there are still a few lonely souls no doubt aching for the warmth of some company, but elsewhere there is a thriving culture of high-latitude surfers. All along the Eastern and Western Seaboards of mainland United States, in Canada, Northern Europe, and the United Kingdom, there are established communities of surfers where summer means only a break from wearing boots, gloves, and hoods, if you're lucky.

A unique bond is formed by hardship. In the same way that communities are lashed together by troubles, or families steeled by tragedy, so communities of cold-water surfers are bound together by the shared experience of pain in pursuit of a few good waves. Given how fickle these locations are, and what you must endure to keep going, you'd have to surmise that the discomfort is part of the reward.

While a shared sense of suffering is one thing, it takes a unique individual to forge a path alone when confronted with the unflinching realities of challenging geography. Consider the case of Freddie Meadows, a Swedish surfer who has dedicated his life to discovering waves in the Baltic Sea. From a surfing perspective, it would be easy to look at a map of the region and dismiss it entirely. But Meadows has dedicated a lifetime to proving that such an approach would be shortsighted. A common surf dream is one in which an idealized wave materializes somewhere you know, somewhere close to home, your local spot perhaps, the nearby lake, →

Later, they donned adapted diving suits, wore wool sweaters under thin neoprene vests, and used rubber gloves intended for washing dishes, all in the quest to keep warm.

Unstad on Norway's Lofoten Islands has become a favorite with cold-water seekers in recent years thanks to its quality waves, beautiful snowy vistas, and the cozy Unstad Arctic Surf camp mod cons, which include a hot tub and sauna. Sea temperatures can range between 37 °F and 59 °F (3 °C and 15 °C), so you may want to check conditions before packing your surf gear.

→ even peeling insistently at the end of your street. Meadows had this dream, and against all odds, he's on a quest to make it a reality. Through the endless nights of Baltic winters, Meadows has studied and traveled the coastline by car, boat, kayak, and on foot. In the process, he has found waves worthy of children's dreams, and he has demonstrated an idealistic pursuit of perfection, discovery, and hope that lies at the root of why many of us surf.

Meadows might not have discovered the most perfect waves on the planet, but they are definitely some of the coldest. Because the Baltic has low salinity compared to other seas, it's less dense and the water gets colder quicker in winter. Water temperatures around the coast of Sweden hover just above freezing in the winter, with an average temperature around Stockholm of just 33 °F (6 °C) in February. Violent winter storms bring short-period, surfable waves to the Baltic, which makes those chased by Meadows some of the rarest and most fickle on earth. He has pursued moments that might never happen again in his lifetime, or anyone else's for that matter, and these moments, unique and never to be repeated, are what elevates the surfing experience.

Dreams Aren't for Everyone

For the most part, these cold-water lifestyles are deeply romanticized. The reality isn't for everyone, and the cold is the great separator. In a world where surfing is more popular than ever, it's perhaps the last bastion of the surfing dream. It's not comfortable or easy, and you can't honestly say it's always fun. But for some, that is part of the reward. The pay-off is worth the pain. ⌒

Index

THE WORLDWIDE
JOY RIDE
p. 4
Photography: Matt Power
mattpowerphoto.com

FEATURES

RIDE EVERYTHING:
THE LONG AND THE SHORT
pp. 28–29
Photography: Popper photo/Getty Images
p. 30
Photography: Tom Kelley Archive/
Freier Fotograf/Getty Images
pp. 32–33
Photography: Cameron Spencer/
Staff/Getty Images

CHASING THE GHOSTS
OF A SURFING DREAM
pp. 154–155, 158–159
Photography: Sebastian Keim
instagram.com/salty_frames
p. 156
Photography: Russell Holliday
russellholliday.com

INCREMENTS OF FEAR IN THE
LAND OF THE GIANTS
pp. 172–173
Photography: Fred Pompermayer
fredpompermayer.com
p. 174
Photography: Stuart Gibson
stugibson.net
pp. 176–177
Photography: Gary McCall
instagram.com/garymccallphoto

STYLE IS EVERYTHING:
THE ART OF SURFING
pp. 210–211
Photography: Ryan Chachi Craig
instagram.com/chachfiles
p. 212
Photography: Emy Dossett
instagram.com/salty_see
pp. 214–215
Photography:
Camille Robiou du Pont
camillerdp.com

SUB-ZERO SURFING
IN THE LANDS OF ICE
AND SNOW
pp. 312–313
Photography: Mark McInnis
markmcinnis.com
p. 314
Photography: Sergio Villalba studio
sergiovillalba.com
pp. 316–317
Photography: Krzysztof Jędrzejak
balticsurfscapes.com

LOCATIONS

ALASKA, UNITED STATES
pp. 188–193
Photography: Mark McInnis
markmcinnis.com

BOCAS DEL TORO, PANAMA
pp. 222–227
Photography: Ryan Chachi Craig
instagram.com/chachfiles

CANARY ISLANDS, SPAIN
pp. 102–107
Photography: Sergio Villalba studio
sergiovillalba.com

CAPE TOWN, SOUTH AFRICA
pp. 68–75
Photography: Alan van Gysen
instagram.com/alanvangysen

CHICAMA, PERU
pp. 234–235
Photography: EyeEm/
Alamy Stock Photo
pp. 236–237
Photography: Isis Monteux
instagram.com/isis.frames

CORNWALL, ENGLAND
pp. 268–273
Photography: Luke Gartside
instagram.com/lugarts

COROMANDEL PENINSULA,
NEW ZEALAND
pp. 48–53
Photography: Rambo Estrada
rambo-estrada.com

CUBA
pp. 228–233
Photography: Makewild
instagram.com/makewild

DAKAR, SENEGAL
pp. 82–87
Photography: Lisa Coulaud
instagram.com/lisa_coulaud

EASTER ISLAND, CHILE
pp. 244–249
Photography: Alfredo Escobar
instagram.com/escobar_photos

ERICEIRA, PORTUGAL
pp. 258–261
Photography: Helio Antonio
instagram.com/helio_antonio

FAROE ISLANDS,
DENMARK
pp. 296–301
Photography:
Sergio Villalba studio
sergiovillalba.com

GHANA
pp. 88–93
Photography: Alan van Gysen
instagram.com/alanvangysen

HEL PENINSULA,
POLAND
pp. 286–289
Photography: Krzysztof Jędrzejak
balticsurfscapes.com

HOSSEGOR, FRANCE
pp. 262–267
Photography: Luke Gartside
instagram.com/lugarts

JAWS, HAWAII,
UNITED STATES
pp. 14–15
Photography: Larry Geddis/
Alamy Stock Photo
pp. 16–19
Photography: Fred Pompermayer
fredpompermayer.com

KERALA, INDIA
pp. 134, 137 (bottom)
Photography: Anna Diekmann
pp. 135, 136, 137 (top), 138–139
Photography: Katie Rae
katieraephoto.com

MADAGASCAR
pp. 108–113
Photography: Alan van Gysen
instagram.com/alanvangysen

MALIBU, UNITED STATES
pp. 178–181
Photography: Jeremiah Klein
instagram.com/miahklein

MARGARET RIVER,
AUSTRALIA
pp. 54–59
Photography: Tom Pearsall
tompearsall.com

MAVERICKS, UNITED STATES
pp. 162–163, 164 (top left), 166–167, 168 (top)
Photography: Ryan Chachi Craig
instagram.com/chachfiles
pp. 164, 165, 168 (bottom), 169
Photography: Fred Pompermayer
fredpompermayer.com

MENTAWAI ISLANDS, INDONESIA
pp. 122–127
Photography: Marc Llewellyn
emvielle.com

NAYARIT, MEXICO
p. 202
Photography: Alfredo Matus/Shutterstock
pp. 203–207
Photography: Emy Dossett
instagram.com/salty_see

NAZARÉ, PORTUGAL
pp. 252–257
Photography: Helio Antonio
instagram.com/helio_antonio

NORTH COAST, SCOTLAND
pp. 280–281, 283
Photography: Luke Gartside
instagram.com/lugarts
pp. 282, 284–285
Photography: Mark McInnis
markmcinnis.com

NORTH SHORE OF OAHU,
HAWAII
pp. 8–13
Photography: Maria Fernanda
mariafernandaphoto.com

NOSARA, COSTA RICA
pp. 216–221
Photography: Callum Morse
saltshots.com

OMAN
pp. 146–151
Photography: Sergio Villalba studio
sergiovillalba.com

PAPUA NEW GUINEA
pp. 42–47
Photography: Ryan Chachi Craig
instagram.com/chachfiles

PICHILEMU, CHILE
pp. 238–243
Photography: Rodrigo Farias Moreno
instagram.com/fariasmoreno

PUERTO ESCONDIDO, MEXICO
pp. 196–199
Photography: Isis Monteux
instagram.com/isis.frames
pp. 200–201
Photography: Maria Fernanda
mariafernandaphoto.com

RAMIN, IRAN
pp. 140–141
Photography: Kingsly Xavier George/
Alamy Stock Photo
pp. 142, 144–145
Photography: Giulia Frigieri
giuliafrigieri.com
p. 143
Photography: Poliorketes/Adobe Stock

SIARGAO, PHILIPPINES
pp. 116–121
Photography: Camille Robiou du Pont
camillerdp.com

SKELETON BAY, NAMIBIA
pp. 76–81
Photography: Alan van Gysen
instagram.com/alanvangysen

TAITUNG, TAIWAN
pp. 128–133
Photography: Matt Power
mattpowerphoto.com

TARKWA BAY, NIGERIA
pp. 94–101
Photography: Oli Hillyer-Riley
olihillyerriley.com

SHIPSTERN BLUFF, AUSTRALIA
pp. 60–65
Photography: Stuart Gibson
stugibson.net

TEAHUPOO, TAHITI, FRENCH POLYNESIA
pp. 34–37, 38 (bottom), 40–41
Photography: Tim McKenna
timmckennaphoto.com
p. 38 (top)
Photography: Vadim Antonov/EyeEm
p. 39
Photography: Fred Pompermayer
fredpompermayer.com

THE SEVERN BORE, ENGLAND
pp. 290–295
Photography: Luke Gartside
instagram.com/lugarts

TOFINO, CANADA
pp. 182–187
Photography: Marcus Paladino
marcuspaladino.com

LOFOTEN ISLANDS, NORWAY
pp. 302–309
Photography: Krzysztof Jędrzejak
balticsurfscapes.com

WAIKIKI, HAWAII
pp. 20, 24 (top)
Photography: Helio Antonio
instagram.com/helio_antonio
pp. 21–23, 24 (bottom), 25
Photography: Bryanna Bradley
bryannabradley.ca

WEST COAST IRELAND
pp. 274–279
Photography: Gary McCall
instagram.com/garymccallphoto

The Surf Atlas

Iconic Waves and
Surfing Hinterlands

This book was conceived, edited, and designed by gestalten.

Edited by Robert Klanten and Rosie Flanagan
Contributing editor: Luke Gartside

Preface by Luke Gartside
Text by Luke Gartside, except for pp. 26–32, 49–53, 69–75, 152–158,
170–176, 178–181, 239–241, 259–261, 302–309, 310–316 by Jamie P. Currie
and pp. 208–214 by Lily Plume
Captions by Luke Gartside

Editorial Management by Anna Diekmann

Design by Isabelle Emmerich
Layout and Cover by Stefan Morgner
Layout Assistance by Antonia Heckenbach

Photo Editor: Francesca Zoe Paterniani

Maps by Michelle Snyder, Quail Lane Press

Typefaces: Goudy Old Style by Frederic W. Goudy,
Neue Haas Grotesk by Christian Schwartz

Cover image by Tim McKenna
timmckennaphoto.com

Printed by Schleunungdruck GmbH, Marktheidenfeld
Made in Germany

Published by gestalten, Berlin 2022
ISBN 978-3-96704-058-6